STREETWISE BUSINESS TIPS

200 WAYS TO GET AHEAD IN BUSINESS, MOST OF WHICH I LEARNED THE HARD WAY.

BOB ADAMS

D1004548

Copyright ©1998, Robert L. Adams.
An Adams Streetwise® Publication. Adams Streetwise® is a
registered trademark of Adams Media Corporation.

This book, or parts thereof, may not be reproduced in any form
without permission from the publisher; exceptions are made for
brief excerpts used in published reviews.

Published by
Adams Media Corporation
260 Center Street, Holbrook, MA 02343

ISBN: 1-55850-778-7

Printed in the United States of America.

J I H G F E D C B A

Library of Congress Cataloging-in-Publication Data
Adams, Bob
Streetwise business tips / by Bob Adams.
p.   cm.
ISBN 1-55850-778-7
1. Small business—Management. I. Title.
HD62.7.A314   1998
658.02'2–dc21   97–39654
                                      CIP

This publication is designed to provide accurate and authoritative information with
regard to the subject matter covered. It is sold with the understanding that the
publisher is not engaged in rendering legal, accounting, or other professional advice.
If legal advice or other expert assistance is required, the services of a competent
professional person should be sought.
— From a *Declaration of Principles* jointly adopted by a Committee of the American
Bar Association and a Committee of Publishers and Associations

Background cover photo courtesy of the Boston Public Library, Print Department.

This book is available at quantity discounts for bulk purchases.
For information, call 1-800-872-5627 (in Massachusetts, 781-767-8100).

Visit our home page at http://www.streetwisebusiness.com

CONTENTS

INTRODUCTION

Every day I get up; I go to work; and I make mistakes. Since I've been making mistakes in twelve different businesses for over twenty years, I've slowly developed a few rules of thumb for trying to keep out of trouble and trying to stay a couple of steps ahead of my competition.

I first presented these rules of thumb on my daily "Streetwise Business Tips" segment on *First Business*, the national television business news program produced by the United States Chamber of Commerce. Positive viewer response and requests for transcripts encouraged me to turn the tips into this book.

It is my hope that this collection of tips will help other hard-working entrepreneurs and business managers avoid many of the problems, pitfalls, and potholes that I have encountered in my continuing search for business success.

—Bob Adams

THE FINICKY BUSINESS OF MARKETING

"Contrary to popular myth, the world does not beat down the door of the better mousetrap developer."

THE BIG SECRET OF BUSINESS!

$\Diamond$

Perhaps one of the best-kept secrets of business is that just about no one is ever really pleased with marketing results!

In some of my earliest businesses, I published newspapers and phone books and personally sold advertising to thousands of small and midsized businesses—and it was very, very seldom that I came across business people who were really thrilled with any of their marketing programs. At the same time, I found many business people who thought there must be some easy "silver bullet" solution that would drive huge crowds of customers to their doors that they just hadn't discovered.

Marketing is an art, not a science. There is no superman MBA or superwoman ad agency executive you can hire who can guarantee you marketing results! The experts don't have all the answers . . . and this is exactly why business owners and managers need to give a huge personal effort to make sure their marketing is working as hard as it possibly can.

IT'S FINICKY, TRICKY, AND TOUGH!

◇

Marketing is finicky; it's tricky; and it's unpredictable. I've seen the exact same ad pull great one day of the week and get no results on another day. I've run ad campaigns on radio and gotten virtually no sales—and other times I've run radio campaigns and doubled sales overnight. I've run huge display ads in prestigious newspapers and gotten no results—and I've run similar ads in much less prestigious newspapers and gotten great results.

A lot of people tend to blame it on the particular media chosen when an ad doesn't pull, but virtually every media can bring in some results. When ads don't work, chances are that one of the very many other variables is to blame: Is the offer attractive enough? Is it eye-catching? Is it believable? Is the timing right? Even the weather can be a factor!

So here's a crucial rule of thumb . . . never spend a lot of money on a particular ad campaign until you've carefully tested it first with a very limited budget.

DON'T LEAVE ADVERTISING TO THE PROS!

◇

After all these years, I still get into trouble with my advertising. To jump-start the sales of the Adams Streetwise software line last year, I bought full-page ads in a major business magazine and got reasonable results. So this year I took the plunge and signed a year-long contract—our first six-figure ad commitment ever. Working with an incredibly talented designer we hired from the ad agency world, we created a much more impactful-looking ad that we thought would at least double if not triple our ad responses.

But when the new ad ran in the 500,000-plus-circulation magazine, we received less than five rebates for this $25 software package. I just blew over $10,000! Worse, I had eleven more ads to go in the contract, and the next ad was already past deadline!

For the third ad we switched back to the terribly cluttered, homespun ad that had worked for us last year, and results shot right up again.

ARE YELLOW PAGES A SURE BET?

---◇---

What about the Yellow Pages? Isn't that a pretty sure bet for advertising results? Nothing is a sure bet for advertising results.

Nineteen years ago I made a sales call on a small service business in St. Paul, Minnesota that was just about to close its doors. The firm had bought an expensive ad in the Yellow Pages that wasn't bringing them results, and the cost literally bankrupted them.

Yellow Pages advertising does work great for many service businesses. But nothing is a sure bet in advertising. And when the Yellow Pages salesperson comes to visit and starts talking about how the ad will cost just a few dollars a day, remember that you've got to make a commitment to pay for the ad for the entire duration of the year.

Before you buy Yellow Pages ads get several years of phone books and note which ads changed from year to year and which ads didn't. This gives you some indication of which ads worked and which ads didn't.

THE "LITTLE BITS" MARKETING STRATEGY

———————— ◇ ————————

U ntil you've found a really successful marketing
vehicle, I think the most important rule of thumb is
to spend a little money here, and a little money there, and a
little money everywhere, until you find the right media mix
for you.

In addition to trying the traditional media, be as creative
as you can.

With my first business, Bob's Rent-A-Bike, I advertised in
local and daily newspapers. No results. Then I bought a $1/8$
page ad in a million-copy-circulation tourist publication. I
was so sure this would work, I didn't wince when the ad rep
told me they had a policy of requiring a minimum of four
weeks of advertising. So I spent $200 on the ads–a good
portion of my life savings at the time. But the ads brought
in only two $5 bike rentals!

Not one to give up, I next tried attaching crude, Magic
Marker drawn posters at campsite bulletin boards offering
mobile bicycle rentals. Bingo! A couple of cardstock posters
sent my sales soaring!

QUICK WAYS TO BOOST PROFITS!

*"Too often in business
we get trapped into equating
sales with profits. Yet there are
many other ways you can
dramatically impact your
profitability!"*

UNDERPRICING KILLS PROFITS!

───────────── ◇ ─────────────

Many small businesses have thinner profit margins than larger firms do because they tend to underprice their products or services. So why not just raise prices? I know the feeling—you're scared that your competition might swoop in like a bird of prey and your customer base might shrivel overnight!

For years we credited much of the success of our best-selling resume book, *Resumes That Knock 'em Dead*, to its relatively low $7.95 price. But my sales manager insisted we could charge more, so when we brought out a new edition, I nervously increased the price by 25 percent to $9.95. What happened to sales? *Unit* sales surged over 20 percent. Total revenue soared 50 percent, and profits skyrocketed!

Still unsure about raising prices? Remember, you can always cut them back. A Chinese restaurant I eat at has rolled the price of its lunch buffet back and forth like a Ping-Pong ball, between $5.95 and $6.25, *four times* over the last two years.

IS THE MARKETING WORKING?

◇

You've probably heard the familiar maxim: "Twenty percent of my advertising brings in 80 percent of my business, but I don't know which 20 percent!" Well, I bet that in your business there is at least one marketing expense that you have a strong suspicion isn't carrying its weight—so cut it and see what happens!

One year I tried cutting three-quarters of the promotional budget for my leading book. What happened? The sales continued to creep upward, and the profit margin of the *entire company* jumped markedly higher.

It's often by eliminating the marketing expenses previously considered most sacred that you gain the most. For example, in the book industry many of the leading publishers have recently stopped participating in the annual national trade show—it simply was costing them too much money for too little return.

THE EASIEST WAY TO PROFITS

◇

Let's say your overall profit margin is 5 percent—not an uncommon level for many smaller firms. But if you can cut your costs by just 5 percent, your profit will double. On the other hand, to get the same increase by boosting sales, you would have to increase sales by 100 percent. Chances are that cutting costs just a little bit would be a lot easier.

To attack your costs take a look at every single expense item starting with the biggest items! Get competitive bids for every product and every service that you buy!

Remember, despite what they may teach you at business school, there is no such thing as fixed costs! Often lease rates, mortgage rates, and utility rates can be negotiated downward, especially if the market has shifted.

REVIEW YOUR PRODUCT MIX!

———— ◇ ————

A seasoned banker once told me about a firm with several highly profitable divisions and one marginally profitable division. The company sold the marginally profitable division, and suddenly the performance of the remaining divisions dramatically improved!

I've tried this! It works! When the economy around Boston hit rock bottom in the late 1980s, I closed my job-advertising newspaper—which was 50 percent of our revenue the previous year. By being able to put all of my energy into the other part of my business—book publishing—it took off, and revenue doubled, more than making up for the newspaper closing.

Even a marginal business or product line that isn't losing money is draining resources—time and focus. Close it and move on!

OUTSOURCE JUDICIOUSLY

———————— ◇ ————————

One of the battle cries in business today is to determine the one thing that your business does best, become even better at it, and outsource absolutely everything else. There is certainly a lot to be said for taking a careful look at every function in your business and asking yourself if you should outsource it. But take a hard look at the numbers before you decide to jump on the outsource bandwagon!

For example, we hoped that by outsourcing the warehousing of our books to our printer in the Midwest we could save lots of money in freight costs. But a careful analysis showed that we would save almost nothing in freight costs and that outsourcing would have nearly doubled our warehouse and handling costs.

FINE-TUNING STRATEGY

"Strategy isn't just a buzzword that MBAs at huge corporations use to sound intelligent!"

HOW TO "STEER" YOUR BUSINESS

◇

How important is strategy? Whether your business is a one-person start-up or a huge corporation, a great strategy is crucial. It's like the steering wheel on a ship. If the ship is in A–1 condition except for a broken steering wheel, it's going to spin hopelessly in circles.

In my twelve different businesses, I've spun around in a lot of circles for lack of a solid strategy. Why is it so hard? Strategy is not *that* complicated! Basically it's just the few key factors that differentiate your business from your competitors'.

But it's easy to fall into traps. Many service business owners proclaim, "My strategy is great service," while CEOs of product companies exclaim, "Our strategy is to produce great products." However, these aren't strategies at all—because their competitors are often making the same claims.

IN WHAT DIRECTION ARE YOU HEADED?

◇

If you're not quite sure where your business is headed these days—or if you're not quite sure if you're taking the right course to get there . . . what do you do? Don't procrastinate! Take action!

Try a complete strategic review. Get together with your key people for a couple of days of undisturbed time—maybe even go off-site or hire a facilitator. For starters, here's a few of the *most basic* issues every company should discuss:

- Future Vision: What kind of company do we want to be five years out?
- Strengths: What aspects of our work do we do well?
- Weaknesses: What aspects don't we do well?
- Markets: What opportunities and challenges loom ahead in the markets we serve?
- Strategic Options: What are our basic alternatives and their implications?
- Selection: Which strategy should we select?
- Implementation: What changes need to be made to implement the chosen strategy?

FIND YOUR UNIQUE STRENGTHS!

───────────── ◇ ─────────────

How do you determine what your strategy should be? How do you weigh strengths and weaknesses? Fifteen years ago leading consulting firms were advising their corporate clients to get rid of any business that couldn't become the market leader. But the truth is that you don't need to be the market leader to successfully compete. But you do need to find some area of strength and some way to differentiate yourself from the competition.

Finding a true strategy—one that really differentiates your business from the competition—may take some energy, but believe me—it'll be worth it.

Here are a *few* possible strategy variables to consider:

- High quality versus low price
- Narrow versus broad product line
- High-tech versus low-tech products
- Trendy versus conservative products
- Brand-name versus generic
- Customized versus standard
- Niche market versus mainstream market

HAVE A BUMPER STICKER STRATEGY!

―――――――――――― ◇ ――――――――――――

Coming up with a great strategy is of course only half the challenge. Getting all of your employees to "buy into" it is the other half. You can't just announce to your staff what the strategy is going to be—I've tried it—they'll forget it the next day. That's why it's so important to get managers (or other key employees if you don't have managers) involved in setting a new strategic course. Have them participate in discussing their vision of the future. Have them create lists of areas of company strengths and weaknesses. And most of all, carefully consider their opinions in setting direction.

Another thing that has worked for me is having what some call "a bumper sticker strategy"—just a few words that capture the spirit of the more detailed strategy plan. A simple "bumper sticker strategy" lets everyone in the entire organization know what the strategy is—and it makes them feel part of it.

DON'T COPY YOUR COMPETITOR'S STRATEGY!

◇

When I was nineteen years old, I decided to start a bicycle rental business on Cape Cod, after I heard about a man earning $150,000 during the summer season renting bicycles. I copied everything he was doing. I bought fifty used bikes and lined up gas stations and motels to act as my rental agents. Then I waited for my profits to roll in ... but no one was renting my bikes. The other guy's strategy didn't work for me. He had new bikes. I had old ones. He had the best locations. I had what was left.

In desperation I tried something different. I put to use my competitive advantage—free use of my mother's station wagon—and offered free delivery of bikes to campsites and motels. Now I had a strategy that differentiated my business from the competition. It didn't matter that my bicycles were old or what price I was charging. I was the only firm *delivering* bicycles.

PLANNING FOR PROFITS

"No matter how small or large your business, you've got to aggressively plan the work—and then work the plan!"

HOW TO REALLY JUMP AHEAD!

———————— ◇ ————————

On a discussion panel, I was recently asked, "Was there a particular turning point when your small business really jumped ahead?" Absolutely. I always made up plans and budgets, but it was about five years into my business before I really began to *proactively use* them.

Before this point in time, my sales projections were miles off and, more importantly, I was always thinking up excuses for making unplanned expenditures, often for advertising that seldom matched my expectations. I'd finish the year way over budget, with profit margins a fraction of what my plan called for.

I learned that a lot of expenditures seem like a great decision if you look at them in isolation–but when you look at them in the context of the whole budget, they often look a lot less enticing.

SHARPLY FOCUS YOUR PLAN!

◇

Too many people equate annual planning with budgeting. Worse, when they budget, they simply extrapolate last year's numbers into next year's plan, perhaps increasing by 5 percent here and 6 percent there.

Big mistake! The annual planning process is your best chance to really *manage* the business—and to get key people to "buy into" the total plan by actively participating.

Even if you're running a one-person business you want to get a few *words* into your annual plans, *not just numbers*. You don't need a full-fledged 100-page business plan—in fact, a big, detailed plan takes focus away from what matters. *What matters* is the few big things that the business is going to strive to do *better or different* next year. The annual planning process should be focused around these few, important changes.

DON'T JUMP INTO BUDGET NUMBERS!

$\Diamond$

Before you start doing any nitty-gritty budgeting for your annual plan, here are the crucial first steps:

1. Review the company's business strategy. Do changing market conditions or heightened competition mean that it's ready for an overhaul?

2. Establish just a few major goals for the next year. These are usually quantitative goals such as to increase sales by 18 percent or to increase profit margins by 15 percent—but they may be qualitative goals such as to improve the quality of a product or customer service. It is very important to have *very few* major goals—otherwise, with too many goals, the company will lose focus and be less likely to hit any of them.

3. If your company is big enough to have departments, have one or several specific goals for each department. To take this one step further, you may want to have specific goals for individual people within each department.

SALES PROJECTIONS NEED EXTRA ATTENTION!

◇

Once you've reviewed the company's strategy and set up company-wide, as well as department, strategies for the next year, then it's time to start cranking out budget numbers.

I always begin with sales, because sales numbers will drive many of the other numbers. Unfortunately, sales numbers, particularly of new products, are difficult to project. So I try to have at least three people, typically a project manager, the sales manager, and myself, work up new-product sales projections together. If you're really unsure of sales projections, consider multiple scenarios based on "weak," "likely," and "good" sales projections.

After we've got the sales numbers, each department works up its budget numbers. Once they're tentatively approved, the controller puts them all together into one big happy plan! But more often than not, I'm not completely satisfied with the overall profit margin, so I'll work with the different department heads to cut costs and drive up the projected earnings.

BENCHMARK YOUR COSTS!

◇

One of the best ways to establish cost goals for annual planning is to benchmark your costs with other firms in your industry. Don't get too wrapped up in the details; focus on the total picture for major categories. For example, if your marketing costs are 23 percent of sales and the industry average is 16 percent, it's time for some cost-cutting. Benchmarking is a great way to get department managers to understand why they need to control costs.

Often industry associations provide standard industry costs, and occasionally they might be mentioned in articles in trade magazines.

You may want to consider hiring a consultant to put together a study of a half-dozen or more firms *very similar* to yours. Being a third party, the consultant will keep each firm's individual numbers confidential by providing only average and median cost information to each company as an incentive for participating. What's worked best for me is when another publisher foots the bill for the consultant, but shares the results with us in exchange for our agreeing to share our numbers.

THE IMPORTANCE OF BEING CHEAP!

"It's more than a coincidence that when I entered the market for local city guidebooks, I decided to go for the low end under the brand name Mr. Cheap's.*"*

PENNY-PINCH YOUR WAY TO SUCCESS!

———————————— ◇ ————————————

One of the most important traits for business success is being cheap! In almost any business, if your cost structure is just a couple of percentage points lower than your competition's, you can have a huge competitive advantage.

When you're starting a small business with no money you learn how to be cheap really quickly. But as your business gets larger and more successful, it's easy to loosen the purse strings and not watch each expense so carefully.

Also, as you hire people it becomes a challenge to get them to adapt the same frugal mindset that you acquired by skimping along in the early days of your business.

BIG COMPANIES ARE GETTING CHEAPER, TOO!

◇

I f you think being cheap is just for small companies, you better think again. More and more larger corporations are using cost control as a competitive weapon.

For example, in New England almost every large regional discount department store chain has gone bankrupt! And who's gaining market share? Wal-Mart!

Talk about cost advantages. The general and administrative costs at one of these large, troubled regional discounters was 27 percent of sales. Wal-Mart's is 15 percent. This cost difference alone can explain the difference between spectacular success and spectacular bankruptcy!

Wal-Mart's costs aren't just lower because they're bigger. They're lower because Sam Walton was the cheapest CEO in America—and by no coincidence, also the richest! Even when Wal-Mart was a fraction of the size of its competitors—so were its costs!

CUT YOUR COSTS WITH ONE CALL!

───────────── ◇ ─────────────

Al Dunlop, known as "chainsaw Al" by some of his detractors for the massive layoffs he's instituted, led an incredible turnaround at Scott Paper by selling off major divisions, repositioning the remaining product lines, creating new marketing strategies, and reviewing every single cost with a fine-tooth comb.

But when you read through his wonderful autobiography, *Mean Business* (which the armchair book reviewers did not appreciate as much as I did), he singles out one phone call that made more difference at Scott Paper than any other action. In this call, Al cut the single biggest cost dramatically—the cost of paper. He didn't just put the paper cost out to bid. Instead, he demanded an unheard-of low price and then offered to give all of his business to the vendor who would meet this price.

SAVE YOUR MONEY AND RENT A DUMP!

◇

Being cheap isn't just a method for looking at every cost ... it's a mindset.

I remember hearing a man talk about a business he was going to start. "I'm going to do everything right. I'm going to get the best equipment; the best location; the best furniture; the best of everything," ... and he's probably had the best bankruptcy, too!

I once went to a bankruptcy auction at an incredibly lavish office complex. There were original paintings on the walls, built-in multimedia screens, skylights–the whole nine yards. I filled up a truck with beautiful furniture that I paid just about nothing for. During the auction a lot of us were wondering what kind of firm this was. It turned out that it was a consulting firm and one of my business school professors had been chairman emeritus. Lots of brains in a business can help you get ahead–but a cheap mindset can keep you out of bankruptcy!

GROWTH BREEDS WASTEFUL SPENDING!

––––––––––––––––––––––– ◇ –––––––––––––––––––––––

As my still-small company grows, I see an attitude of complacency to costs growing along with it—and I can fully appreciate how large corporations can get pulled into wasting money needlessly.

For example, I hear people saying things like: "A corporation of our size needs to look like this . . . or ought to be doing that. . . ." When you hear this kind of talk, you can bet that someone is trying to justify something that *has no justification!*

Another explanation for needless expenditures that amazes me goes something like this: "Well, we spent $3,000 on company sweatshirts, so I figured $200 for a subscription to a newsletter is a drop in the bucket."

One day I found my marketing people had become almost totally focused on conveying the right corporate image in our trade ads as opposed to trying to sell product! Again the explanation was that at our growing size we shouldn't be so concerned anymore with directly generating sales!

MEETINGS THAT MOTIVATE!

"By nature meetings are dull, dreary, and dreaded—but with a little effort you can create meetings that people look forward to and that will drive your company ahead!"

MEETINGS THEY LOVE; MEETINGS THEY HATE

〈◇〉

I love to talk at meetings. I love to lay out grand strategies, lofty goals, and ambitious initiatives.

But guess what? My managers hate it! They're tired of hearing me talk!

What they really want to do is *participate* in the meetings. They don't just want to give a couple of words of feedback at the end of the meeting—they want to play a core role in formulating decisions. I find that when I don't go to the extra effort to set up a forum so that they can *easily* join the discussion, then I end up dominating the meeting—and I don't get my managers' full support.

But I've found that if my managers really feel they've participated at meetings, they leave feeling empowered, invigorated, and fully committed to whatever course we have chosen to pursue.

GET THE COMPETITIVE JUICES FLOWING!

◇

There's nothing like a look at the competition to get people excited! I've found that you can lay the foundation for a great interactive meeting by starting with a close examination of just one of your competitors. Ask people, "What do they do well? Not so well? What can we learn from them?"

I've found that taking a look at the competition is a particularly good way to get managers involved in the discussion, even when they represent very diverse functions. "How does this company use its credit policy to compete? Does it keep deep inventories? What's its cost structure? Where does it spend its marketing dollars?"

I've found that even when reviewing a much weaker or smaller competitor, you can always find at least one thing that they are doing much better than you!

HAVE A MICRO-FOCUS!

◇

Again and again I find myself starting meetings with a very broad focus, saying, for example, "Any new marketing ideas today?" Then everyone says to themselves, "Not another boring meeting." Why do I fall into the trap of having meetings that lack focus? Frankly, because I just didn't take a few minutes to prepare a more specific topic.

But when I do give the meeting a more specific focus—for example, "How can we increase the retail shelf presence of product A?"—then people jump into the discussion, and the meeting moves ahead.

Focus makes meetings work. Focus on one product, or one customer, or one supplier, or one market niche.

Even at the giant retailer Wal-Mart, where hundreds of managers crowd into an auditorium for weekly meetings, they might focus on the sale of one product type, like beach apparel, at just one store. Then at the end, they try to see if any conclusions they reach can be applied more broadly.

USE ANOTHER IDEA SOURCE!

◇

The worst way to get my managers to buy into an idea is to announce it myself. The best way is to have it emerge from one of them during a group discussion.

But I find that my managers don't stay up late at night the way I do, looking for exciting new ideas to discuss at meetings. So sometimes I'll take a middle road.

Instead of just presenting something as my idea, I'll quote a stimulating short passage from a book or magazine article.

My managers are a lot more receptive to hearing suggestions from a third-party expert, and an outside voice helps liven up the meeting. Besides, this gives me more incentive to look for fresh ideas myself!

SO YOU MISSED YOUR BUDGET AGAIN!

◇

Variance analysis—comparing actual sales, costs, and profits with the budget—is a basic managers meeting topic. But it can also be explosive! I've learned the hard way that berating managers in a group setting for missing a budget is a big mistake! Remember that with even half-dedicated managers, the numbers speak for themselves!

So keep the focus on what can be done differently in the future! The past is done—so discuss it only to learn, not to criticize!

Last spring our sales were way off budget. But our profits were slightly above target, because our costs were way under budget. My first tendency at budget meetings was to focus overwhelmingly on the sales problem. But the more I thought about it, the more I realized that we had achieved new breakthroughs in cost control and that we needed to examine how we had done this so we could make sure we continued to do it in the future!

NEWSLETTERS TURN BUYERS INTO CUSTOMERS!

"I kicked, screamed, and dragged my feet when my marketing manager wanted to try a newsletter. 'Why not just send product flyers?' I asked. But they've worked for us and a lot of other companies, too!"

WILL THEY BUY FROM YOU TOMORROW?

◇

So they bought your product yesterday, but will they buy it tomorrow? In many markets the substantive differences between products have narrowed to the point of insignificance. Hence, your ability to build a relationship with people who buy your products is more critical than ever. And newsletters can help build relationships. They can show customers how to get more value out of your products, perhaps by showing how other customers are finding new uses for them or, in the case of resellers, by showing new ways to merchandise them.

You want customers to know as much about your products and services and your firm as they possibly can. And you want to keep your firm fresh in their minds. If you can do this, they are going to be much more likely to do business with you again, even if a competitor is offering the same product or service at the same price.

CREATE PRODUCT EVANGELISTS!

———————— ◇ ————————

Especially in its early days, when it dominated the emerging market for personal computers, Apple Computer was phenomenally successful at creating product evangelists. These were people who not only liked Apple computers, they loved them, and they loved them so much they told everyone they knew to go buy one!

Newsletters can help create product evangelists by building a bond with your product users. You may also want to send newsletters to "key influencers"–people who are in an unusually good position to be able to recommend your product to many others.

For example, part of the success of our *JobBank*™ career books is attributable to how widely and favorably they have been recommended to job hunters by college placement counselors and librarians–to whom we often send mailings.

AVOID THE HYPE!

――――――――――― ◇ ―――――――――――

One of the reasons many newsletters work is that people read them—no small feat when one considers the typical mail volume at most businesses. The reason people read them is that they think they might find something useful or interesting—not just a blatant sales pitch.

For example, the leading publisher in the book trade, Random House, has a newsletter that is as well-read as some of the industry trade magazines. People love the chatty, informal, no-hype style. And the newsletter has tremendously added to its credibility and readership popularity by occasionally recommending books published by competing firms. Like many other newsletters today, the Random House newsletter is also available free-of-charge on the Web.

CRACKING TOUGH ACCOUNTS!

◇

My marketing manager loves newsletters because in his earlier twenty-year career as a retail buyer, newsletters got him to place orders, but fancy brochures and flyers went quickly into the wastebasket.

In my experience I've had mixed results mass-mailing newsletters to cold prospects, opening up just a few new accounts. On the other hand, though, I find that newsletters work well as *one* part of the sales mix, when you are already calling or visiting a critical, but difficult, new account.

Sometimes I find that buyers at larger accounts drag their feet picking up a new product until they feel it's already a well-established success. And a newsletter is a perfect vehicle to communicate the success of your products to potential buyers.

SIDE BENEFITS OF NEWSLETTERS

◇

Newsletters are great not just for customers, but also for getting employees, distributors, commission sales reps, the media, and other third parties excited about your firm. I'm often surprised to hear that even many employees learn important new information about our company through the newsletter.

I've also found that the job of newsletter editor is a great motivator in and of itself. I know one of our newsletter editors felt that creating the newsletter was the most exciting part of his entire job—no big surprise since he was in charge of the newsletter and the rest of his job consisted of being one of many assistant editors on a large editorial team.

HAPPINESS IS POSITIVE CASH FLOW!

*"Cash flow, not profits,
is the lifeblood of your business.
Project it, monitor it, and
manage it well before
serious trouble starts to brew."*

DON'T JUST ADD THE NUMBERS—MANAGE THEM!

———————————— ◇ ————————————

I f you're like me, before you dream of going into a new business you have dreams of big, fat profits. But once you're in business, you dream instead of positive cash flow.

Crucial in controlling cash is having a detailed cash-flow projection, updated at least every month. But don't just add up the numbers—*manage* the numbers. Often by careful management you can realize huge cash savings without changing the course of the business.

One of the first candidates for cutting that I'd look at would be inventory. I found that when I was running into cash shortfalls, I could cut over $300,000 in projected inventory purchases with minimal risk of stockouts, even when my business was only doing about $5 million a year in sales.

PAYABLES MANAGEMENT BOOSTS CASH!

––––––––––––––– ◇ –––––––––––––––

Payables can be just as important as receivables in boosting cash flow.

Know the payment norm in your industry—not just the stated terms, but when suppliers actually get paid. Then delay your payments to the slow end of the accepted norm. We used to print most of our books with a firm that gave us 90-day terms; then it got a new CFO and insisted on faster payment; we now pay them in 60 days . . . *the few times that we still use them.*

Some suppliers offer "dating," meaning extended terms— a few even offer outright financing. The ultimate solution is to eliminate your inventory entirely by buying on consignment, meaning that you don't even own the goods until you either sell them or use them in your manufacturing process.

I used to distribute the books of smaller publishers on a consignment basis, paying them only after the books were sold.

EVALUATE YOUR PRODUCT MIX!

◇

Y ou can change your product mix to boost cash flow—
and perhaps improve your return on investment at the
same time. Consider dropping those products that tie up
cash the longest and replace them with faster moving items.

I visited a manufacturer of high-performance powerboats
ranging in size from 16 to 33 feet. Just prior to my visit, I
was surprised to hear, the company had discontinued its
king of the fleet, a critically acclaimed 65-foot sport
fisherman. The owner's brother explained to me that while
the 65-foot yacht was selling well and had good profit
margins, it tied up money for too long—because of its slow,
custom production process.

There are few business people who have the discipline to
drop their flagship product because of a lousy return on
investment—but this doesn't mean that you can't profit by
being one of them!

TURN ASSETS INTO CASH!

———— ◇ ————

Of course, you can always sell assets to improve your cash position.

You can sell your receivables (called factoring) to a commercial finance firm. It'll usually be more expensive than traditional receivables or working capital financing—but it does create cash and cleans up your balance sheet. If you own your building, you can sell it and lease it back—some of the largest and richest corporations in America have done this—so why not you, too?

You can also put together a bundle of all of your used equipment and get a leasing firm to buy it and lease it back to you.

New accounting rules may force you to disclose leases on your financials, but to most bankers lease liabilities appear less onerous than traditional debt, and by turning assets into cash, you may not even need to borrow at all!

FOCUS ON THE GROWTH BUSINESS!

— ◇ —

If you're trying to grow a small business really fast or if you're in serious financial trouble, you'll need a more extreme solution to finding more money.

You can always try to take in investors, but if you're growing fast or if you're in trouble, you'll dilute your ownership much less if you can wait until later.

What I have done on several occasions to finance fast growth is to sell a product line or a part of the business that is highly profitable, but doesn't have the best growth prospects. For example, last year I sold our small career-magazine group to a subsidiary of the Washington Post Company. A steady and profitable business, the magazine group had contributed as much as 50 percent of our revenue in their early 1980s, but only about 5 percent of our revenue in 1995, as our other businesses had rapidly outpaced it.

PUBLICITY FOR EVERY BUSINESS

"I made a big mistake not seeking publicity for every single business I ran, including my early, tiny businesses."

THERE'S ALWAYS A PUBLICITY ANGLE!

———————— ◇ ————————

When I went into the book business, it was a no-brainer to spend a lot of effort getting publicity—every other publisher was doing it. But I made a big mistake not seeking publicity for all the other tiny businesses that I had previously operated.

No matter what business you are in, there is a publicity angle that you can capitalize on! For example, let's say that you sell life insurance in a small town—how can you possibly get publicity? Well, you could offer to write an article for the local paper helping people determine what level of insurance coverage is appropriate for their situation.

One of the great values of publicity, especially print publicity, is that you can save a copy of the article and show it again and again to current and prospective customers.

TARGET YOUR PUBLICITY!

◇

How can you get publicity? Look for the media that your customers use and that might be interested in your story. For example, for a local service business it'll be easier to get publicity in your local newspaper than in the major metro paper—and you'll reach the same people you want to, anyway.

Develop a story angle that might appeal to each media outlet. For example, if you are pitching your restaurant to a TV station, offer to demonstrate your cooking.

Get a list of contacts—the appropriate editor at newspapers and magazines or the specific show producer at radio and TV shows. Mail a one-page pitch letter explaining why your story will interest their audience, perhaps also including a press release, photos, or a video. Follow up with a phone call—then get ready to meet the press!

THE BIG MEDIA ISN'T ALWAYS THE BEST!

---◇---

Develop a strategy for getting publicity. Even if you do your own publicity, it does cost time and energy.

Target the media that is most likely to benefit your business—not necessarily the most prestigious media. Back in 1981, I first published a job-hunting book called *The New York JobBank*. The *New York Times* ran a wonderful feature story, and I even appeared on NBC's *Today* show and was featured in *People Magazine*. But the publicity that sold the most books by far was a very short article that appeared in the relatively downscale *New York Post*.

For many product firms the best place to get publicity is going to be in a trade publication; for many local service firms, the best place to get publicity is going to be the local newspaper.

HOW PUBLICITY HELPED BUILD IBM

◇

Always be ready to talk to the media.

In 1955 *Time Magazine* assigned a staff writer, Virginia Bennett, to write an article about office automation in America. She first visited Remington Rand, famous at the time for its UNIVAC computer. But its executives weren't available for interviews.

On the way back she passed a window display of computers at another firm and tried to get an interview there. At this company the founder was an absolute stickler on how the public—and especially the media—should be treated at the door. Within minutes Bennett was interviewing a very forthcoming Tom Watson, Jr., CEO of IBM. A major cover story followed, equating IBM's products with the advance of civilization.

In his autobiography, Watson portrays this publicity coup as a major turning point in his battle to overtake Remington Rand and to clinch the lead in the race to computerize corporate America.

"NO COMMENT" IS NO GOOD!

◇

How do you respond to the media during a crisis?

It's really tempting to say, "Call me back later." Or simply not return calls. But this is the worst approach. When the media reports that you did not return phone calls, it appears to many people—rightly or wrongly—that everything the media says is true and that there are no good explanations.

Another approach is to downplay the actual seriousness of a problem—also a big mistake. Intel tried to downplay what truly was an obscure error on one of its microprocessor chips. Nonetheless, the media had a field day.

On the other hand, the classic success story in handling a media crisis occurred during the Tylenol scare. The executives in this situation were very up-front and highly accessible, and they quickly developed and unveiled a massive corrective action plan.

CHEAP MARKETING TRICKS

"Often in marketing it's the cheapest and most creative concepts that really bring home the bacon!"

COUPONS AND REBATES REALLY PULL!

$\diamond$

Almost every business should at least consider discount or rebate coupons. You can pay to have them distributed in newspapers, in magazines, or by direct mail. Or what's even cheaper and more effective is to personally hand them out to customers most likely to respond to your offer, such as at the street corner in front of your business, at homes near your business, at nearby businesses, or at trade shows.

Better yet, try mailing some coupons to existing customers or include "next purchase" coupons when you ship customer orders.

One of the beautiful aspects of coupons is that they can be "quick and dirty" to design and print because their selling point is price, not image. Don't hesitate to be generous with your coupon offer: today's price-conscious consumer is unlikely to respond to just a 5- or 10-percent discount.

Also, I have found low-value, like $5 or $10, rebates to be highly profitable because people buy your product *intending* to mail in the rebate—but few ever *actually bother* to send it back.

FREQUENT-BUYER PROGRAMS WORK GREAT!

◇

Businesses ranging in size from major airlines to local car washes rely heavily on frequent-buyer programs for good reason: They work!

The most common approach is to give customers a card that is punched or recorded in the computer, resulting in a free or reduced-price product or service offering after a specified number of regular-price purchases. For example, ten haircuts may net one free one.

Another approach is to give regular customers a discount on every purchase upon presentation of their "frequent buyer" card.

The real power of a frequent-buyer program isn't just retaining customers with a standardized discount program. The real power is that it gives you information about customers that tells you when and what they're buying—so you can target mailings or phone calls to specific customers. And it tells you when customers aren't buying, so you know when you need to lure them back.

NEW-CUSTOMER OFFERS BREAK THE ICE!

◇

Y ou don't have to be in business for too long before
    you figure out how hard it is to get new customers!
Ads that simply describe your service or product often
produce disappointing results. That's because you need to
do more than just attract customers—you need to steal them
away from the competitor who is currently serving them!

Consider *new-customer offers:* one-time-per-customer
specials to lure new clients into your fold: special pricing,
buy-two get-one-free offers, free-gift-with-purchase offers,
extended warranties, money-back guarantees.

In a service business, consider free estimates, free
appraisals, free first consultation, or a free trial period.

Even most *lawyers* will offer a first-visit-free consultation.

CONTESTS GET ATTENTION!

———— ◇ ————

ontests are a great, cheap way to build excitement and visibility for your business. People love contests—just witness the phenomenal success of TV game shows.

A contest can be as simple as "guess the number of jelly beans in the jar" or as complicated as deciphering an encrypted treasure map.

Make your contest fun, make it wacky, and be sure to talk it up! It's a great way to build that elusive and all-powerful "word of mouth" advertising by getting your customers and employees excited about your business. And if you play it right—with a couple of phone calls and a simple press release—you ought to be able to get some free publicity both when you announce the contest—and when you announce the winner!

CHEAP SIGNS BRING BIG SUCCESSES!

———— ◇ ————

I n marketing you just never know what will work best until you try it. When I went on a bookstore tour last year, my company and every bookstore tried lots of different marketing approaches. We spent a lot of money on local newspaper, magazine, radio, and direct-mail advertising. Stores passed out fancy invitations and arranged elaborate in-store displays. Most everything we tried produced some results—but the response was inconsistent and unpredictable. For example, with the exact same ad in the same daily newspaper in Columbia, South Carolina, we got a great response when it ran one day, but absolutely no response when it ran another day.

However, overall, the single most successful promotional approach cost nothing. At the Joseph-Beth bookstore in Cincinnati my event was announced on a flyer in the bathrooms—in a *carefully chosen strategic* place where it could not be missed!

MANAGING FAST GROWTH

"Fast growth is one of the most exciting times to be running a business—but I've found it's a much more dangerous and tricky time than you might first assume."

ADD SYSTEMS AND PROCEDURES

$\diamond$

As a business grows, you won't be able to spend as much time personally checking over all the details. So you need to formally delegate as much work to others as you possibly can. Set up systems and procedures to ensure that critical work is getting done the way you want it done.

For example, when my business was starting I personally dropped everything when a new book arrived from a printer and did a quality check. Now that we're publishing 150 new books a year, quality checking is not a good use of my time. So I have two people, from the department that orders the printing, check every shipment and fill out a quality report form before we ship it out.

At first I was reluctant to delegate this work (and, for that matter, just about every other job I've ever delegated). But guess what—they now do a more rigorous job of quality checking than I used to—and they've learned to be just as stingy with the company's money! Yesterday they convinced a book printer to give us a 50 percent discount because the red color on the cover was a slightly different shade than ordered!

FAST GROWTH BURNS CASH!

◇

Ironically, if your business is profitable and growing very quickly, your cash needs may grow quicker than the money you generate from operations—especially if you sell on credit or carry inventories. It's not impossible for even a highly profitable but fast-growing company to run out of cash and be forced into bankruptcy!

This is why all businesses, but particularly growing firms with inventory and receivables, need to carefully project and continually adjust their cash-flow demands. In my book publishing business, we look at an uncomfortable cash-flow projection about once a year—typically in the summer when payments and sales are slowest. But so far we've always avoided serious trouble by making cutbacks or speeding cash inflow before the problem becomes serious.

In a fast-growing business, you've got to take the time to very carefully and thoroughly do monthly updates of your cash-flow projection or you're going to run into trouble.

EVALUATING GROWTH OPTIONS

◇

Because often the limit to growth is money, a fast-growth business needs to view both growth options and discretionary expenses from the perspective of which will have the fastest return on investment (R.O.I.).

For example, I was very willing to accept much lower profit margins in distributing the books of other publishers because I had virtually no investment! Since I held them on consignment, I didn't have to pay for the books until I sold them.

When considering offering new products or services, you need to give particular attention to return on investment. But you should also think about return on investment when considering expenses. What's the return on new desks or new rugs for the office—probably nothing! Which marketing campaign should you try? Which one do you think will have the fastest return on investment?

FAST-GROWTH PEOPLE ISSUES

$\Diamond$

A fast-growth business means lots of hiring. I often underestimate the amount of time it takes to hire people—especially the right people—and to get them up to speed. Writing job descriptions, posting ads, sorting through resumes, interviewing, orientation, and training all take time. But I've found if you do your hiring in batches, it can take a lot less time!

Current employees, especially more senior ones, sometimes feel undermined by new hires. So show them you appreciate them, explain why the new position is needed, and try to involve them in the interviewing process. I have found the hard way that salary information often leaks out—so make sure the pay for new hires is not out of line.

One of the harder issues to confront is that some managers won't be able to keep up with fast growth. The person who supervised two people in your warehouse when you started out may not be able to manage your current warehouse staff of forty. In a fast-growing company, even one weak manager can slow down the entire firm.

WHEN IS FAST GROWTH TOO FAST?

———————————— ◇ ————————————

Sustainable fast growth must be "controlled" fast growth! No matter how fast you are growing, you need to have time to keep your financial projections up-to-date. Your projected cash flow should allow enough room in your credit line at the bank to allow for some unforeseen or underestimated expenses—which often happen in fast-growth situations.

You also need to watch that your profit margins are not slipping significantly—a frequent occurrence at very fast-growing firms where focus is often more on sales than profits. Watch both your overall profit margin as well as your gross profit margin (sales less only the costs of the goods sold or the direct costs of the services you provide).

Importantly, being in control of fast growth is more than having a bunch of nice financial statements and projections. You need to feel comfortable about the overall situation. You particularly need to feel comfortable with the ability of your key managers; you need to feel that the quality of your products or service is not slipping; and, perhaps most of all, you personally should not feel "burned out."

MAKING WORK FUN!

"To have a really happy workforce, you've got to do more than pass out party hats and serve birthday cake."

BEYOND PARTY BALLOONS AND BIRTHDAY CAKES

———————————— ◇ ————————————

Over the years, I've tried a lot of things to make work a crazy, fun, and wild place. I've tried playing rock music in the morning, having group lunches at noon, throwing parties later in the day, and arranging for sports after work. But whatever crazy thing we try, it loses its novelty after a while and people tire of it. Yeah—they're good now and then to bring your office alive, give people a chance to have some fun together, add a human face to your management style, and as another way to show people that you care about them.

But I find that the bottom line is that people come to work because they want to work—not just to play games and have silly parties. Beyond the money, people expect more and more out of their work today. They want to contribute; they want to see that their contribution is making a difference; they want to learn; they want to grow; and they want to feel that they are part of a successful enterprise that is making a difference in the world. It's achieving these kinds of satisfactions that really keeps people coming back to work every day—not just the party balloons and birthday cakes.

MAKING WORK REWARDING

◇

H ere are some specifics that you need to make sure you are doing to help ensure that their work is satisfying to the people who report to you:

- Today's workers at all levels want to know *why* they are doing something. Don't just say, "Drop everything you're doing and rush this shipment out." Instead, take two minutes to explain why.
- Today's workers want to work hard and have pride in their work–but they need appreciation and recognition for their contribution. Be generous with compliments.
- Today's workers want input and accessibility to their managers–but many shy away from giving input unless you make it easy for them. Small group meetings where you ask for suggestions are a good way to get people involved.
- Today's workers want to feel that their work is making a difference. Explain why their work matters. Tell them success stories about people who use your products and post press clippings on the bulletin board.

HELPING EMPLOYEES PROGRESS

◇

For many employees it's important to feel that they are always growing, learning, and progressing. With the few employees at small firms and flatter management structures at larger ones, it's a challenge to fulfill this need. But it's important you do—because often it's the best employees who most feel the need to learn.

Recently our Web master—the person who runs our World Wide Web site—left for another job. The manager of this area wanted to get a qualified candidate from the outside because none of the four internal candidates had all the necessary skills.

On paper he was right: the best candidate would be from the outside. But I want our company to go out of our way to retain people, give them new challenges, and make work fun for them. So we divided the Web-master job among several people, giving them all a great chance to grow and learn something new. In the short term it might be inefficient—but in the long run a highly motivated staff is priceless!

REMEMBER, YOU SET THE TONE!

◇

Recently one of my managers pointed out to me that when I, as owner of my company, make a comment on people's work, they pay a lot of attention to it—something I tend to forget.

Another time, another manager told me that when I'm in a good mood it helps boost up everyone else—but when I'm not, it darkens people's days.

As a manager at any level, you've got to try to project a positive attitude no matter how crummy a day you are having—and you've got to go out of your way to be sure your comments have a positive effect on people. I've even got a little yellow stick 'em posted on my computer reminding me to always be positive!

First thing in the morning is a great time to pass some positive energy and appreciation on to others with an enthusiastic greeting and a little small talk.

And at the end of the day, no matter how rough it's been, I always try to wrap up with people on a positive note.

HOW OFTEN SHOULD YOU PARTY?

◇

My experience is that about once or twice a week during working hours is the right time to spend on those silly, frivolous activities.

Here's some of the diversions that have worked for us:

- Friday morning bagels.
- Friday afternoon theme parties.
- Occasional lunch outings such as mini-golf, bowling, or billiards.
- Seasonal decorations at the entrance.
- Company crosswords and contests.

I've tried a lot of elaborate events outside of working hours, but they've almost always been disappointing. Attendance was mixed; people would arrive late; and managers felt pressured to attend.

A high-level technical manager told me that the single thing that impressed him the most about our company during his first month was that he went bowling and played miniature golf during company hours.

BUILD YOUR BUSINESS WITH TRADE SHOWS

"In many industries, trade shows can really accelerate building your business without your spending a whole lot of money."

BEYOND WRITING ORDERS

———————— ◇ ————————

There are many compelling reasons for attending trade shows. Don't view them as just an opportunity to write orders. In fact, in many industries, few orders are taken on the trade show floor. Here are other reasons companies attend:

- To get new leads.
- To build relationships with customers.
- To launch new product lines.
- To seek distributors or sales reps.
- To enhance the firm's reputation.
- To "pre-sell" customers before sales visits.
- To check out the competition.
- To get industry media coverage.
- To attend seminars.
- To network.

PREPARATION DETERMINES THE OUTCOME

◇

A successful trade show requires advance preparation. Clarify goals and objectives–these are not always obvious. If this is a show that you have attended in the past, think about what you want to do differently or better this time around. Develop a plan and a budget, as well as a detailed checklist of what needs to be done at what point in time.

Set up appointments with the people you want to see before the show begins–at some shows, many people are fully booked in advance.

The better trade shows sell out fast, and first priority goes to past attendees. So get your booth application in as soon as possible to increase your chances of getting a good location.

I've also found that despite the rules for booth allocation, it doesn't hurt to get on the phone and push for a better booth location.

STEAL THE THUNDER!

---

ome booths at trade shows are jammed with people while others are empty. Traffic flow at your booth is not simply a matter of luck. Here's what you can do to get them to your booth:

- Mail invitations in advance.
- Send press releases to industry publications.
- Offer free giveaways or prize drawings.
- Offer show specials or new account "openers."
- Give a workshop or seminar for attendees.
- Have "action" activities at your booth.
- Serve food or drinks.
- Have large, enticing signage.
- Greet people in the aisles.
- Dress in costume.
- Provide comfortable seating.

TRADE SHOWS FOR PENNIES

◇

It doesn't have to cost a lot of money to exhibit at a trade show. In fact, my total costs including travel, lodging, and exhibit space for the first major national show we attended was only $600.

Many national shows offer smaller spaces or even tables for smaller exhibitors for very low prices. Some offer special deals on travel and accommodations.

A simple 2 × 3 foot poster along with a few product samples proved very effective for making our first tabletop display.

If you want to look more polished, you may want to consider a portable display. A small, single booth or tabletop commercial display is inexpensive to ship and can be set up at virtually any convention without hiring union labor.

BEWARE THE TRADE SHOW DRAGON!

— ◇ —

I t's easy to break your trade show budget and end up kicking yourself for the rest of the year.

A few years ago we bought a large professionally made trade show exhibit that we couldn't wait to show off at the annual book industry show. The closer we came to exhibit time, the more our excitement built, and the less attention we paid to our budget.

By the time we were done we ended up spending $60,000—double our original budget. The display looked polished and slick—but did it do us any good? One of my sales reps said, "You spent a lot of money, but now your display looks just like the other publishers'."

Now, even though we own a professional-looking exhibit, we build our bigger trade show displays with plastic milk crates! We find it's cheaper to buy the milk crates and throw them out after the show than it is to ship our big exhibit and pay union labor to set it up. And you'd be surprised how many favorable comments we get on the milk crates!

IMPROVING COMMUNICATION

"Better communication can really help get your team moving together."

THE BIG COMMUNICATION REVOLUTION!

— ◇ —

A few months ago I had lunch with one of my favorite professors from Harvard Business School, Bill Bruns. Bill told me about a fascinating research project he was working on to study internal communications at some of Europe's largest and most progressive companies. He concluded that one modern wonder was far more important than any other in improving communication at these companies. And I bet you can't guess what it is!

Cheap air tickets. That's right! Not e-mail. Not intranets. Not video conferencing. In fact, Bill found that the more managers communicated electronically, the more pressing became the need for face-to-face meetings.

AVOID E-MAILING EMOTIONS!

———— ◇ ————

E-mail, intranets, faxes, voice mail. They're fine for accelerating the transfer of factual information. But when your communication involves any emotion—such as the expressing of different opinions—a face-to-face meeting is by far the best bet, with a traditional, interactive, phone conversation a distant second choice. Believe me—I've irritated enough people to know!

Why is face-to-face communication so important? As we get more efficient at communicating facts electronically, we tend to forget how much emotion we convey through body language and voice tone. For example, as I say with words that I disagree with someone, my tone, my posture, my smile, and my eye contact may at the very same time be saying, "I value and respect your opinion and enjoy working with you . . . even though I disagree with you on this point."

TALK IN THEIR TERMS!

— ◇ —

Experts on sales techniques suggest that you talk with prospective customers at the same rate of speech that they talk with you, because people usually like to listen at the same speed that they talk.

Similarly, I find that different people have different preferred methods of communication and that people often send messages by the way they like to receive messages. Some people prefer to communicate in person; others leave a lot of voice-mail messages; others use e-mail; others use memos; others, maybe the company intranet.

When we hire people from much larger corporations, we find that they often alienate people by at first relying too heavily on memos. In any company or department, communication will be stronger and people will work together better if you can standardize communication methods.

SHUT UP AND COMMUNICATE!

—— ◇ ——

So much of communicating successfully is listening successfully. And I have to admit this is something I'm not always so good at myself!

But it is a skill that can be learned. I recently put together a group of eight consultants to create a software package, *Adams Streetwise Managing People*. It was fascinating to me that despite their different backgrounds and areas of expertise, the consultants all emphasized the importance of listening in solving a vast array of problems. For example, they often suggested that you first tackle people problems by listening to the employees' perspective and then paraphrasing it back to them, both to be sure you *understand* what they said and to emphasize that *you care about* what they said.

WHY MEETINGS MATTER!

—————— ◇ ——————

For the first few years of Adams Media, I tried to avoid holding meetings like the plague—I thought meetings were the ultimate sign of bureaucratic paralysis at larger corporations.

Then I discovered that meetings had some important purposes other than just getting things done—and suddenly I was holding meetings all the time! Meetings can make people feel part of a group. And participative meetings give people a feeling that their opinion can be heard, and that it counts!

A lot of problems in communication come about when employees feel that someone else is either not listening to them or does not value their opinion or, worse, does not value them. And today's workers expect to know what is going on at their company, how their work fits into the whole picture, and what the future holds in store.

CHOOSING INCENTIVE PLANS

"The right incentive plan properly implemented can drive your business ahead like a rocket ship. But if expectations increase faster than actual payouts—watch out for trouble!"

INCENTIVE PLANS PULL COMPANIES TOGETHER!

◇

Years ago the only employees offered incentive pay were sales personnel, piece workers, and top executives. Today most large corporations, and many smaller firms, offer an incentive package to all of their employees.

Some kind of incentive pay is an important part of any compensation plan. Incentive pay shows appreciation and creates a sense of participation in the company's well-being that straight salary dollars, no matter how large, don't convey. A well-designed incentive-pay plan can also help pull people together, help point them in the direction you want them to go, and give that extra push that every company needs in today's competitive environment.

PROFIT-SHARING PLANS ARE COMMON

—— ◇ ——

Profit-sharing plans are probably the most widespread incentive-pay programs at larger corporations. They are generally company-wide and made available at least to all full-time employees. Usually the company will contribute a small percentage of its pre-tax profitability to a pool, which is then divided among eligible employees. Division is typically prorated according to the base salary of each participant. Profit sharing is generally done on an annual basis. At some firms profit sharing may be directly contributed as pre-tax dollars into a retirement program, such as a 401K program.

Profit plans work best at more established firms with relatively steady earnings. The criteria for the profit plan must be carefully defined in advance.

PROFIT PLANS DON'T ALWAYS WORK

—————————— ◇ ——————————

The advantages of a profit-sharing plan include: It pulls people together since everyone is on the same plan; it gets people to focus on profitability; and its cost to the company goes up and down in sync with pre-tax earnings.

The disadvantages include: It echoes the base salary; it does not take into consideration performance during the year; it is focused on a single objective.

For smaller companies with erratic earnings, profit-sharing plans can frustrate and irritate employees by creating expectations that are not fulfilled each year. I switched away from a profit-based incentive plan because I found that a small payout level, following a year of weak profitability, made a low morale situation even worse.

INCENTIVE PROGRAMS AWARD ACHIEVERS

L ast year we switched to an individual bonus incentive program, where the annual payout is determined by a subjective evaluation of each person's performance.

The advantages are: Unlike a profit-sharing plan, we can dramatically differentiate the payout given to a star performer versus a weaker one; we can differentiate between an individual's performance and the company's performance; and there is complete flexibility for a significant one-time payout if an employee has an extraordinary accomplishment that may not be repeated in future years.

The disadvantages include: The payout is subjective, and employees may feel that they deserve a higher pay-out; it can be divisive when, all too often, a top performer tells other people what a big bonus they got; employees may focus more on "looking good" than on working to increase corporate profits.

MANY OTHER INCENTIVE OPTIONS

———— ◇ ————

I n addition to profit sharing and bonuses, here are some other incentive options:

- In salary-at-risk plans, which I don't recommend, employees receive their full base pay only if performance meets minimum goals, but a larger payout is possible.
- Gain sharing, popular at some manufacturing firms, provides for a portion of increases in efficiency to be shared with employees.
- Stock or options are available at many public companies, but are less practical at private ones.

I've successfully used cash awards for specific achievements, such as cost-cutting ideas.

Some plans have multiple goals with a percentage of the payout determined by how well a person performs on each objective. While I highly recommend incentive-pay plans, design and implement yours carefully! All too often incentive programs backfire when they fail to meet employee expectations.

BUILD CUSTOMER LOYALTY!

"It takes a lot less money to increase your retention of current customers than to find new ones—but I know I don't give it as much effort as I should because it does take a lot of energy and effort!"

STRATEGIZE AND PLAN FOR LOYALTY!

◇

Do you even have a specific plan for building customer loyalty?

I bet you haven't given it as much thought as you should–because to tell the truth I need to give it more effort also.

If you currently retain 70 percent of your customers and you start a program to improve that to 80 percent, you'll add an *additional* 10 percent to your growth rate.

Particularly because of the high cost of landing new customers versus the high profitability of a loyal customer base, you might want to reflect upon your current business strategy.

These four factors will greatly affect your ability to build a loyal customer base:

1. Products that are highly differentiated from those of the competition.
2. Higher-end products where price is not the primary buying factor.
3. Products with a high service component.
4. Multiple products for the same customer.

MARKET TO YOUR OWN CUSTOMERS!

◇

Giving a lot of thought to your marketing programs aimed at current customers is one aspect of building customer loyalty.

When you buy a new car, many dealers will within minutes try to sell you an extended warranty, an alarm system, and maybe rustproofing. It's often a very easy sale and costs the dealer almost nothing to make. Are there additional products or services you can sell your customers?

Three years ago my house was painted, and it's now due for another coat. Why hasn't the painter called or at least sent a card? It would be a lot less expensive than getting new customers through his newspaper ad, and since I was happy with his work I won't get four competing bids this time. Keep all the information you can on your customers and don't hesitate to ask for the next sale.

USE COMPLAINTS TO BUILD BUSINESS!

—— ◇ ——

When customers aren't happy with your business they usually won't complain to you—instead, they'll probably complain to just about everyone else they know—and take their business to your competition next time. That's why an increasing number of businesses are making follow-up calls or mailing satisfaction questionnaires after the sale is made. They find that if they promptly follow up and resolve a customer's complaint, the customer might be *even more likely* to do business than the average customer who didn't have a complaint.

In many business situations, the customer will have many more interactions after the sale with technical, service, or customer support people than they did with the sales people. So if you're serious about retaining customers or getting referrals, these interactions are the ones that are really going to matter. They really should be handled with the same attention and focus that sales calls get because in a way they are sales calls for repeat business.

REACH OUT TO YOUR CUSTOMERS!

◇

ontact ... contact ... contact with current customers is a good way to build their loyalty. The more the customer sees someone from your firm, the more likely you'll get the next order. Send Christmas cards, see them at trade shows, stop by to make sure everything's okay.

Send a simple newsletter to your customers—tell them about the great things that are happening at your firm and include some useful information for them. Send them copies of any media clippings about your firm. Invite them to free seminars. The more they know about you, the more they see you as someone out to help them, the more they know about your accomplishments—the more loyal a customer they will be.

LOYAL CUSTOMERS AND LOYAL WORKFORCES

◇

Building customer loyalty will be a lot easier if you have a loyal workforce—not at all a given these days. It is especially important for you to retain those employees who interact with customers such as sales people, technical support, and customer-service people. Many companies give a lot of attention to retaining sales people but little to support people. I've been fortunate to have the same great people in customer service for years—and the compliments from customers make it clear that they really appreciate specific people in our service function.

The increasing trend today is to send customer-service and technical-support calls into queue for the next available person. This builds no personal loyalty and probably less loyalty for the firm. Before you go this route, be sure this is what your customers prefer. Otherwise I'd assign a specific support person to every significant customer.

One last thing—don't tell your customers your 800 line phone number is for orders only!

CONTROL YOUR TIME!

"I bet I could have cut back on many of the seventy-, eighty-, and ninety-hour weeks that I've put in over the years, if I'd been more systematic and rigorous in managing time!"

GET AGGRESSIVE ABOUT MANAGING TIME!

— ◇ —

Time and money are both very important in business. Yet, like me, many business people tend to give a lot more specific thought as to how to spend their money. Too often, how we spend our time is only thought of in terms of "What am I going to do today?" or "What should I do next?"

Just as a well-run business should carefully develop a strategy to determine how to spend its money, an effective businessperson should carefully develop a strategy to determine how to use his or her time.

Just as a well-run business follows a budget in spending money, an effective businessperson should also follow a budget (or schedule) in spending time.

PRIORITIZE YOUR TIME!

---◇---

The first step in effective time management is not to develop a schedule, but instead to develop a time strategy. The time strategy should be based on a short list of time priorities.

You start by identifying the Number one way you can most increase profits by use of your time; then the Number two way; then the Number three way; etc. This short list of time priorities forms the foundation for your time planning for every week of the year.

These time priorities may be identical to key parts of your company strategy or they may be different. For example, if your company strategy is based upon excellent customer service, spending lots of your time in customer service may *not* be the best use of your time if you have a terrific customer-service manager.

NARROW YOUR FOCUS!

— ◇ —

Focus is crucial for time management, and the fewer priorities you focus on at once, the more productive you will be.

After you have your major time priorities for the year established, you should allocate them by week or by month. Like it or not, a lot of our time each week is going to be eaten up by nonstrategic items that we have no control over; hence it is important to limit the number of strategic time goals we have for each week. So even if you have ten strategic time goals for the year, you may want to focus on no more than one or two of them in any given week.

For example, in a particular week you may plan on working on your Number one time objective, let's say planning improvements for the company's major product line, and a secondary goal, let's say re-evaluating the dealer marketing program, but no time on other secondary time goals that you plan on tackling during other weeks.

SET ASIDE UNINTERRUPTED TIME

———————— ◇ ————————

Every week you should make up a detailed time plan, which you modify each day as needed. Except in times of crisis, try to make sure day-to-day issues don't push your strategic time priorities off your schedule.

Generally your major strategic time priorities will involve such activities as planning, thinking, and developing ideas. More so than day-to-day issues, such activities require big blocks of uninterrupted time.

Constant interruption kills any hope of effective time management. One way to avoid interruption is to make it clear that when your door is closed you are not to be disturbed. Another is to have regular meetings, such as every week, with the people that you interact with the most and insist on saving nonpressing issues for these meetings.

AVOID MY TIME TRAPS!

◇

These are some "time traps," all of which have plagued me, that you should guard against:

- Spending a disproportionately high amount of time in the offices where the most congenial people are, as opposed to where the most important issues are.
- Wasting too much time getting daily updates on routine activities as opposed to waiting for a more meaningful weekly summary.
- Jumping too eagerly into the routine, more straightforward work and putting off the more complex and difficult work.
- Not starting the more important work first thing in the morning.
- Not bothering to make up a schedule for each day.
- Overscheduling–scheduling each day so tightly that it is impossible to stay on track and the schedule quickly becomes meaningless.

WORKING WITH PROBLEM EMPLOYEES

*"As my father often reminds me,
you can't expect all of your
employees to be as hard-working
as yourself; but with help,
virtually all employees
can do a good job."*

EMPLOYEES WANT TO WORK!

—— ◇ ——

I've found that you can turn around the performance of *almost* any problem employee.

Virtually everyone wants to succeed at work, give it their best effort, and get along with people, too. When shortcomings or problems arise, I find that they can almost always be overcome with some additional coaching or with a positive, but frank, discussion of the issues at hand.

As much as possible, you want to leave people with the feeling that you are helping and supporting them, not reprimanding them. And if you have to say anything at all negative to an employee, say it in private.

EVERYONE HAS STRENGTHS AND WEAKNESSES

◇

Often I find that when employees appear to lack the skills to perform their work, there is another factor affecting their performance. Maybe the real problem is sloppiness. Maybe they did not get a clear definition of what their job is. Or maybe they need a little coaching to get acclimated to a new task.

If the problem is a *lack of skills*, perhaps a coworker, a professional seminar, or even a book or software package could help.

Everyone has strengths and weaknesses. If you can identify weaknesses, you can usually work around them. For example, if you have an otherwise great sales manager who can't keep organized, you can assign her a highly efficient assistant.

PICKING UP THE PACE

———— ◇ ————

Some employees do the job—but they do it *too slowly.* Almost always, with a little patience and with a benchmark against which to compare performance, you can help get slow-performing employees up to speed.

For nonprofessional jobs you can create standards. For example, warehouse workers may be expected to pack 150 boxes per day; data-entry people to process 75 orders; sales people to make 50 phone calls.

Standards don't work as well for professional jobs, but you can set goals for each project. For example, you can expect a software engineer to finish part of a program within a week, or a graphic artist to create a brochure within three days.

ELIMINATING SLOPPINESS

◇

Sloppiness is one of the most pervasive workplace issues. For the first incidence or two of sloppiness, kindly point out the problem, without comment.

If the sloppiness proves to be recurrent, sit down with the employee outside the earshot of coworkers. The employee probably doesn't see their work as being sloppy—everyone takes pride in their work. So rather than make generalizations like "your work is a mess!" cite some specific examples.

Sometimes the employee will say, "But these are isolated cases!" Don't get pulled into an argument by responding directly. Instead, explain how important their work is to the company and how important it is to try to eliminate all errors and sloppiness.

THE THORN IN YOUR SIDE

◇

An employee who performs their job responsibilities fine, but nonetheless is difficult to manage *can make your life miserable!*

Address the underlying issue, not just the telltale symptoms, such as an increase in tardiness or an occasional outburst at a meeting. Take the problem employee out to lunch, build a rapport, and find out what the real issue is.

Often you'll find that the employee no longer feels appreciated. This especially happens when a new hire challenges their stature, when they are passed up for a promotion, or when they hear that another employee is earning more money. But the underlying cause may not be work related, such as a medical problem or pressures from home.

Occasionally you will encounter a malcontent who just isn't going to be happy anywhere—so let them be unhappy someplace else!

DATABASE MARKETING

"While no marketing method is a sure bet, chances are terrific that some type of database marketing is going to work really well for your business."

DATABASE MARKETING IS FOR EVERYONE!

––––––––––––––– ◇ –––––––––––––––

Whether you're a partner in a consulting firm, a housepainter, or president of an international conglomerate, database marketing is crucial for your success.

Database marketing can be simple or sophisticated. The key is that instead of just having a mailing list of prospective customers or a single list of current customers, you can use a computer to evaluate and manage the information more precisely.

For example, you may want to send a reminder mailing to every customer once a year; a monthly mailing to more active customers; and even place a phone call from time to time to your very best customers.

TIER YOUR PROSPECT BASE

◇

We generate hundreds of thousands of dollars in revenue every year selling reference books to libraries at very little cost by almost exclusively using database marketing.

While there are tens of thousands of libraries in the country, we have learned from experience that main public libraries with budgets over $25,000 are by far our best target customers. So we mail to this relatively small group of just over two thousand libraries, six times a year.

Less promising prospects, like college libraries and branch libraries, we mail to just once a year.

This reflects a primary rule for database marketing— spend most of your money hitting your best customers repeatedly, but save a little to experiment with new target groups.

We also make follow-up phone calls to our very best prospects like the largest library systems and to previous customers who didn't order this year.

USE A MIX OF MARKETING VEHICLES

◇

Historically, database marketing relied overwhelmingly on direct mail. Then increasingly telemarketing has been used. And now there are a slew of alternatives to consider, including e-mail, fax, and the World Wide Web. Be cautious of legal restrictions that in the U.S. prohibit companies from sending unsolicited faxes to people or companies with whom they don't have a business relationship.

Particularly for closing sales for higher-ticket goods or services, a combination of several different contact methods may work best.

For example, you may first send a direct-mail piece to "warm up" a prospect and then phone to get an appointment where you try to close the sale in person.

Or in a direct-mail piece you may refer the prospect to a World Wide Web site, a fax-back number, or an e-mail address where the prospect can get more information without hesitating because they don't want to talk to a salesperson just yet.

FANCY AND EXPENSIVE DOESN'T ALWAYS SELL!

◇

Again and again, I've learned in direct-mail campaigns that fancy and expensive doesn't always mean better results. Also, once you get into four-color printing the start-up costs are high, so it is very expensive to test even small quantities.

Make your mailing pieces professional and clean—but don't go overboard.

Generally a one-page letter, a two-to-four page flyer with two colors at the most, and a business reply card are all you need for an effective mailing.

Avoid using mailing labels—address the envelopes yourself or have a mailing house do it by computer.

Make sure you have a "call to action" in your letter—like a free evaluation, a free gift, or a limited-time deep discount.

Test all the variables in small quantity mailings, giving extra emphasis to testing different mailing lists and different offers.

TEST! TEST! TEST!

———————— ◇ ————————

I n database marketing, changing even a small variable can wildly change your results. So once a mailing works for you in test quantities, do the exact same mailing to the exact same mailing list in larger quantities.

When you do tests, isolate one variable at a time. For example, in a direct-mail test last summer for our *Adams Streetwise Small Business Start-Up* software, I had three people write totally different letters, each of which we sent to two different magazine subscriber lists. We even included a snappy four-color flyer and a generous $10 rebate on a $40 software package. We carefully marked each response card so we could track sales. The results were easy to analyze. All six variants of the test produced almost identical results: *Nothing*—a response of less than $1/10$ of 1 percent for a net loss of over 90 percent of our costs. That's why you always do test quantities first!

PROGRAMS EXCITE PEOPLE!

*"Highly publicized
company-wide initiatives
can really rally your troops!"*

BEYOND SHOUTING "WORK HARDER, WORK FASTER!"

◇

Company-wide initiatives focused in a single direction are a great way to get people in motion, move the company forward, and create a feeling of unity. You just can't keep screaming at people, "Work harder, work faster"— believe me, I've tried! But when you give people a particular realistic but challenging goal and focus—then you're communicating to them in a way they can relate to. I've also found you can't motivate people month after month with the same goal, like "Let's boost profits yet again!" However, by varying the program and having more limited objectives— that's how you get people's attention!

Announce your new program at a big company-wide meeting. Have splashy signs around the office. Remind everyone continually about the program. Apprise people of the progress. And celebrate its success!

SPEED 'EM UP!

---◇---

One of my favorite company-wide programs is a "Speed" program that can simultaneously cut costs, increase sales, and ratchet up profits. I find that even the best employees tend to overwhelmingly focus on quality and thoroughness, with much less regard for speed and timeliness. But in today's fast-changing, hypercompetitive world, you've got to focus on speed and timeliness, *in addition* to quality.

A few years ago I insisted that we move from a five-day turnaround on shipments from our warehouse to a twenty-four-hour turnaround. At first I was told it was simply impossible. But I knew it wasn't, because a few of our competitors were already doing it. So I made it a major company initiative with lots of positive encouragement, and we made it happen in almost no time at all! Fast order turnaround directly led to more sales by keeping our wholesalers and retailers better stocked with our products.

In the future, I hope to rapidly speed up our software development schedules, by leaving out many of the "nice" but seldom-used features that customers don't care about.

GET EVERYONE THINKING SALES!

◇

One of the things that just about kills me about running a business is how so many employees forget that everything we do needs to be tied in to sales. One example is when my marketing department creates "image" ads with not even an intention of adding to sales. Or when someone in the operations department groans because a huge batch of new orders means lots more work for them.

When I jump up on a desk and shout, "Sales are our sole reason for existence!" people simply think that I'm crazy. But I have had more luck with company-wide sales programs, especially when we focus on one product at a time. This last spring we published a book called *Small Miracles*, and I made an extra effort to get everyone in the whole company excited about it. The accounting department stuffed statement mailings with flyers for the book. The credit department was especially lenient on orders for this title. The operations department made shipping this book an extra-high priority. Even the receptionists and customer-service people talked up this book! The result: ten weeks so far on the *New York Times* Expanded Bestseller list!

QUALITY PROGRAMS NEED SPECIFICS!

◇

Quality programs are probably the most popular type of company-wide initiative. Frankly, I've never used one because I find that speed and efficiency is more what I need to push at our company. And I think it's important to remember that you need to carefully identify the program that will most benefit your firm—not just offer a quality program because everyone else is doing so.

Quality programs—especially those that lack specifics or go on indefinitely—can easily backfire. One large company I visited had a huge 10 × 80 foot quality banner mounted above the production floor, but it meant nothing to the employees, who had seen it for years and had become particularly cynical about recent company cost-cutting.

On the other hand, I visited a boat manufacturer that set up a highly successful quality-control program. This firm decided to distribute in cash to employees any money budgeted but not actually used for warranty repair work, and it soon slashed the number of boats returned for defective workmanship.

CREATE A HIGH-EFFICIENCY OFFICE!

— ◇ —

Too often we tend to think of efficiency as something relegated to the production process. But with so much of today's work being done in offices, not factories, there's a lot to be gained by focusing on efficiency in the cubicles. Today, when people from different functions are interacting more and more, you will get much more mileage by making efficiency programs company-wide.

Specific steps like a two-hour morning quiet time and encouraging cross-functional interaction at all levels have really helped us. But what's also helped us is creating a general awareness of efficiency. For example, in the past we've had one or two people who would sometimes wander from one department to the next gossiping with anyone they could find. Today this seldom happens—not so much because a manager might address the individual, but more because most people in the office *want* to focus on getting their work done.

ELIMINATE THE OVERHEAD!

"Overhead, like the government, tends to just grow and grow. To reduce overhead takes incredible discipline and a willingness to risk civil war with all affected employees."

OVERHEAD IS A THREAT TO YOUR SURVIVAL!

◇

A low-cost structure is essential for being competitive, and low overhead is crucial for this. Overhead costs don't directly make your product or deliver your service. They don't directly benefit your customer. Overhead just adds to your cost structure and makes you less competitive.

Overhead is like government bureaucracy—it just grows and grows. And the more it grows the harder it is to see its benefit. Once you add an expense to overhead it's hard to take it away.

Unfortunately, too many employees love overhead! They love nice desks; they love new computers; they love new buildings; they love deep carpet; they love nice offices! But all these trappings of success are just that—traps—and each and every overhead expense threatens every company and every person that works there.

GET RID OF THE OFFICE!

---◇---

There was one move I put off making for several years that by itself chopped our overhead to shreds and gave us a huge competitive advantage. I delayed moving to a commercial office.

For four years I operated my book publishing business out of my basement apartment. This wasn't just a one-person office. I had up to seven people working there. And we also used it as a warehouse. I'd have neighbors move their cars so semitrailers could back down the driveway. I'd open the large kitchen window to load books in and out. I remember one night waking up to find that a pile of boxes with books had fallen on top of me while I slept.

My MBA friends laughed at this low-budget business setup, but today no one laughs at the 100 percent equity I hold in my $10 million business.

DON'T GET SEDUCED BY TECHNOLOGY!

◇

I t's incredibly easy to get seduced by the latest advances in high technology and by expensive equipment that you either don't need or could make do with a less expensive version of.

Years ago when I was running a busy newspaper sales office, I was shocked to see how expensive multiline phone systems were. So by our reception desk on the first floor I installed six single-line phones for incoming calls and installed six matching extensions on our second floor, using an intercom to announce incoming calls. It looked very crude, and it was appallingly unprofessional, but it worked, and it saved us a lot of money.

Today, the backbone of our accounting system is still an ancient IBM system 36 computer. But I was a lot less embarrassed about this relic in our office when I saw one in operation at the leading wholesaler in our industry.

TRY SELECTIVE UPGRADING!

◇

Personal computers and related software can be a significant expense for a small business and even for a larger one. Often a firm will decide to unilaterally upgrade all of their PCs and software. But there is very little volume savings on PCs and usually not too many savings on software–in fact, I've seen some software site licenses that are more expensive than buying multiple copies off the shelf.

So I would suggest that you look at who really needs the latest and most powerful PCs and who really needs the latest version of an expensive software package. Usually software versions are backward and forward compatible anyway.

But don't skimp by not buying the appropriate software licenses. You could be subject to massive fines and embarrassment if you don't have a software license, not just for each package, but for each PC the software is installed on.

TURNING GARBAGE INTO GREENBACKS

— ◇ —

Most companies spend a lot of money getting their waste hauled away. But my company *makes* a lot of money getting its waste removed!

I would like to tell you that this was a result of my brilliant insight, but that would simply not be true.

As we went through one of our perennial cash crunches a couple of years ago, I got everyone together and said, "Don't panic, we're not going to cut jobs—but we do need everyone's help to cut costs. And we'll give some small cash awards for the best suggestions."

Well, sure enough, most people panicked anyway and told one another we were about to go out of business. But they still liked the cash award idea, and we got lots of great suggestions—including the "money from wastepaper" plan from some of the hourly guys in the warehouse. These fellows directed us to a paper converter who would not only pick up our paper waste for no charge—but also pay us thousands of dollars for it.

COMPETE WITH THE GIANTS!

"When you're faced with a new, bigger competitor, you can survive, prosper, and succeed—but it can't be 'business as usual.'"

NEW COMPETITION REQUIRES NEW STRATEGIES

◇

In one industry after the next, super-sized national and international corporations are driving smaller firms right out of business. What can you do to survive? You've got to completely reconsider your business strategy.

One effective strategy is to refocus your entire business on one specific niche. For example, a local lumberyard faced with some national competitors may be better off focusing exclusively on contractors. You could really get to know the needs of the contractors in your area, and the national competitor's huge television advertising campaign aimed at consumers would not threaten your business.

In developing your strategy, consider your relative strengths and weaknesses. The big national firms have obvious strengths such as financial clout and purchasing power—but every smaller firm has its own particular strengths, too!

CONSIDER THE HIGH END OF THE MARKET

———————————— ◇ ————————————

W hether you're running a retail business, a product business, or a service business, your best bet in competing with a big national firm may be targeting the high end of the market.

The high end of the market generates fewer dollars and hence will probably not be a primary focus of a national firm. Also, the larger firm is likely to have strong cost and financial advantages that put you at a perhaps insurmountable disadvantage if you try to compete in terms of price.

In the toy market, for example, the relatively small high-end chain F.A.O. Schwartz, as well as many higher end independents, have prospered despite the low prices and huge toy inventories of national players like Toys 'Я Us, Wal-Mart, and Kmart.

ADD ADDITIONAL SERVICES

◇

One of the most common suggestions you'll get on how to survive against big national competitors is to emphasize service. If you take service to mean simply saying "hello" and smiling at every customer, this alone will not ensure your survival.

But if you take emphasizing service to mean providing additional *services*, well, then we're talking a whole different ball game! For example, some hardware stores faced with a new Wal-Mart across the street, which sells many products for less than the hardware store can buy them for, have survived by offering services like lawn mower repair, skate sharpening, and key duplicating.

Ten years ago, there were thousands of independent business people selling computers. Today, those independent resellers that have survived—and there are plenty of them— have done so by emphasizing customization, installation, and service.

BUILD POWERFUL RELATIONSHIPS

◇

Another way to survive in a world of giant businesses is to build affiliations.

By belonging to a chamber of commerce or business organization, for example, you may be able to get preferential rates on insurance and other services.

Wholesalers and manufacturers are increasingly supporting their small-business customers with programs such as financing, advertising, and information systems.

Some smaller product firms that are otherwise extremely competitive are finding it difficult to get their products distributed and sold—so they seek an affiliation with a national product firm that sells the smaller firm's products for a percentage of the revenue.

One of the most clever affiliations I've heard about concerns the owners of two independent bookstores who found they were each spending too much of their time talking to publisher's sales reps. So each bookseller began seeing only half of the publisher's reps, but bought books for both stores at the same time.

COMPETE ON YOUR OWN TERMS

—— ◇ ——

Despite my advice, if your overall strategy finds you in direct competition with big national firms, remember that they have strengths that you don't have—but you can succeed if you compete on your terms, not theirs.

Study their business intently. Block any of their moves that threaten you. And then tackle them—when they're not expecting it.

For example, let's say you're selling a product through retail outlets and you hear that your competitor is about to launch a gigantic multimillion-dollar ad campaign. You can't possibly match their ad spending, so don't try—instead, give the retailers an immediate deep discount (like "buy five, get one free") to clog up the retail channel and fill shelf space.

Later, when they're not running a big ad campaign, is when you might want to do your own advertising effort.

HIRING TOP PERFORMERS

"If you're trying to achieve excellent levels of performance in your organization, it's going to be a lot easier if you hire terrific people in the first place."

RE-EVALUATE THE JOB BEFORE HIRING

—— ◇ ——

I f you're going to grow your company or achieve excellent levels of performance in your business unit, it's going to be a lot easier if you hire top performers to begin with, rather than if you have to be constantly pushing and pulling average performers to new levels.

Before you even place the first "Help Wanted" ad for a vacant position, you should do the following:

- Re-evaluate the mix of responsibilities assigned to the position.
- Consider if the current people are assigned to the most appropriate positions.
- Prioritize the "must have" qualifications for the job; the important qualifications; and the helpful, but less important, qualifications.

DON'T JUST RUN A "HELP WANTED" AD

◇

Where should you advertise to attract new help?
"Help Wanted" ads and employment agencies, both of
which can be expensive, are obvious places to start. Here's a
few other suggestions:

- Encourage current employees to mention the opening
  to friends. Consider offering, like many other
  companies do, a referral bonus.
- Put up a sign on your building—we've attracted many
  warehouse workers this way.
- Especially for professional and technical positions,
  advertise on the World Wide Web—for example, at the
  job posting site operated by Adams Media (called
  careercity.com) over 125,000 jobs are posted from
  thousands of different companies across the United
  States
- You can also access resume databases. Careercity, for
  example, has over 17,000 current resumes. Resumes on
  the Web tend to skew toward technical people, but the
  breadth of resumes being posted is gradually widening.

QUICKLY CATEGORIZE ALL APPLICANTS

◇

Over the years I've wasted huge amounts of time in the hiring process. So how does one become more efficient? Here are a couple of strategies I've adopted:

- Immediately sort all candidate resumes into five categories, from the very best to the completely unqualified, and keep every resume sorted this way during the entire hiring process–moving resumes from one category to the next when new information makes this appropriate.
- Spend as little time as possible in the early stages of the hiring process eliminating the clearly weaker candidates from consideration, but spend as much time as possible in the final stages of the hiring process sorting out the more subtle differences between the very strongest candidates.

PHONE INTERVIEWS SAVE TIME!

◇

One of the biggest time-savers in hiring is the phone interview. The best part about phone interviews is that there is no established protocol for minimum length. If you don't like the candidate's first few responses, you can simply say, "That's all I have for today," and move on to the next candidate.

Some hiring experts–like Peter Veruki, my coauthor for *Adams Streetwise Hiring Top Performers* and currently Director of Placement at Vanderbilt's Owen School of Business–stress the importance of allowing the candidate advance notice to arrange a phone interview. But personally I prefer the candidate who's ready to drop whatever they're doing and talk to me on the spot.

During a phone interview, I like to get quickly to the knockout questions like availability, willingness to relocate or travel, and especially salary. If the candidate won't give me a salary range over the phone, I won't have him or her into the office for an interview.

BEYOND THE STANDARD REFERENCES

◇

How do you choose between top job candidates? References are a starting point, but I find that references supplied by candidates are becoming less useful every year—companies concerned about legal liability refuse to give references altogether, and many supervisors sugarcoat the performance of even employees that they've just fired. I put much more weight on whatever kind of reference I can find on my own—maybe from a coworker, a former customer, or someone who knew the candidate through a trade association.

I also like to simulate the actual work that the employee will perform. Typing tests, accounting tests, and sales and management decision-making scenarios have helped me make hiring decisions.

Even if the employee will report to me, I always get plenty of input from others, which also makes people feel more accepting of new hires.

CREATING A BIG IMAGE FOR A LITTLE BUSINESS

"You can make a small business appear very big to the people who matter to you without spending a whole lot of money."

WHAT IS YOUR FACE TO THE WORLD?

◇

I t's tempting to show off—to lease the corner office in a prestigious office tower and decorate it with designer furniture. Don't do it! It won't make you any money. And when your business is in a slow cycle with angry creditors calling, you'll wonder, "Did I spend just a little too much money on the office suite?"

For most small businesses, in fact, you're much better off just running your business out of your home.

Unless you are operating a retail store or expect clients to regularly visit your office, your face to the world will be your products, your services, your literature, and your marketing.

Running a business out of a home is increasingly well accepted. Be sure your business room looks totally business, and ideally arrange for a separate entrance.

Of course, you can always try to meet at the customer's location or, for a really image-conscious customer, you could even rent a meeting room.

HOW DOES YOUR BUSINESS SOUND?

———— ◇ ————

How your office *looks* is irrelevant if your customers are not going to see it. With most business being done on the phone or on your customer's premises, what's more important is how your business *sounds*.

Is your business phone always answered in the same professional manner? Is there music or any other nonprofessional background sound? What happens when your phone is unattended? I wouldn't have just an answering machine or voice mail; I'd spring the extra couple of bucks each month for a really professional-sounding answering service—your phone is your lifeline to the world.

Whatever you do, don't pull the stunt of trying to change your voice to make it sound like there is more than one person in your office. It's usually transparent and instantly destroys your credibility.

PROJECT A CONSISTENT "LOOK"

— ◇ —

A little bit of effort in designing your "corporate look" can go a long way in building your image. At the least, you should use the identical typeface for your company name (your logo) on your letterhead, your faxes, your envelopes, your business cards, your ads, your catalog, and your literature. If you want to get fancy, you can add a piece of art or a splash of color to your logo—but it's not necessary. Observe what other companies do or get a book showing award-winning stationery designs. Get ideas—but don't risk copyright or trademark infringement by directly copying from others.

I heard a story about a new designer at a book publishing company who wanted to redesign the catalog, which had for years sported a bright, but unappealing, stripe down the spine. But the sales manager said, "No way—it is that stripe alone that allows booksellers to quickly pull the catalog out of a big stack."

IT'S AN ELECTRONIC AGE!

◇

Even if you're running a surfboard rental shop or a housepainting business, an e-mail address should be part of your business mix today. Even if just a few of your customers want to communicate with you by e-mail, the minor expense will quickly pay for itself.

What about your own Web site? An e-mail address is much more important than having your own Web site. But an address on the World Wide Web will further add to the professional image of your business.

It doesn't have to be fancy. The biggest gain for most small businesses will generally just come from the fact that they have a Web address at all. The site itself could be very simple. For most tiny service businesses one page would be fine, with a couple of nice photographs, clean graphic layout, and some text about their business.

HOW ABOUT A NEW NAME?

◇

No way around it, people judge your business by its name. My current business was incorporated as Bob Adams, Inc.—*not* a particularly inspiring name. "I'm Bob Adams of Bob Adams, Inc.," I would say. And potential customers would think, "So what!"

So two years ago I changed the name of the company to Adams Media Corporation. The book publishing part of the company I called Adams Publishing. We quickly discovered there were several other companies called Adams Publishing, which brings me to another issue—trademarks. A significant percentage of small businesses run into trademark issues with their business name—especially if it's a clever one. Ideally you should do a trademark search and at the least make sure no business anywhere near you is using either the same or a highly similar name.

Meanwhile we called the computer and on-line area "Adams New Media." Unfortunately, this ran into trouble, too, because the employees in the book area felt they were now considered to be the second-class citizens of Adams "Old" Media.

WHEN IT'S TIME TO FIRE

"You can't expect to successfully manage a business unless you are prepared to fire employees whose performance is consistently unsatisfactory."

DON'T PROCRASTINATE FIRING!

◇

No one enjoys firing people. But getting someone out of the organization who just can't do the job or who is a de-motivator can give a huge boost to the performance of the business.

The general tendency, mine included, is to put off the decision to make a firing, because it's not an easy issue. But procrastination just makes it worse for you, for the organization, and perhaps even for the employee, who may get a fresh start somewhere else.

How much time should you give a failing employee to improve his or her performance? I like to take into consideration the employee's service with the company. Also, firing a long-term employee will be more likely to impact other employees than firing a relatively new hire.

OFTEN YOU CAN BOOST PERFORMANCE

◇

Before you fire someone, give them some chance to improve their performance. I've been pleasantly surprised to see some failing employees suddenly turn around their performance after a stiff warning.

Before you fire someone, create a substantial paper trail in case you end up in court. Keep detailed notes of their performance problems and be sure to issue at least one, and ideally several, written warnings. If possible, identify specific targets that the employee is not hitting, such as a sales quota of $1,500 a day.

An employee who starts receiving written warnings may likely find another job and quit anyway, which dramatically reduces your chances of getting sued.

PLAN FIRINGS IN ADVANCE

◇

Once you think it's unlikely the employee's performance is going to dramatically improve, and once you've considered the legal ramifications, go ahead and carefully plan out when and how you are going to do the firing. Don't torture yourself with second thoughts and guilt—just do it.

Think it through in advance. Plan to have at least two managers at the firing so you have a witness, if necessary. Write out a script so you don't say something that you don't mean that could be legally damaging.

Don't be overly dramatic. Generally I'd let the employee finish out the workday or even the week and allow them to bid farewell to everyone in the workplace.

HOW TO SAY "GOOD-BYE"

$\Diamond$

What do you say when you fire someone?

Get to the point quickly and briefly explain why they are being "let go."

Summarize the main reasons and remind them that they have been warned about their performance.

Then go into the details—such as when you expect them to clean out their desk, severance pay (if any), continued health-care coverage they may be legally entitled to—and hand them their final paycheck.

Show the employee sympathy, but not empathy. Do not waiver or change your mind. Most of all, do not say anything positive about the employee's work performance—this will increase your chances both of getting sued and of losing a suit.

AVOIDING TERMINATION SUITS

◇

While in the United States there aren't any laws that take away the right to fire employees for "just cause," including unsatisfactory quantity or quality of work, for all practical purposes you do face significant legal risk every time you fire someone.

It is illegal to fire someone on the basis of sex, age, race, religion, or handicap. In fact, about 80 percent of the population can find some umbrella under which to claim discrimination.

Discharged workers find it hard to accept that their performance was poor and place tens of thousands of suits each year.

Here are four ways to protect yourself:

1. Document weak performance.
2. Consult with an employment attorney before the firing.
3. Don't pay severance unless the employee waives the right to sue–in the United States, workers over age forty must have three weeks to sign a waiver.
4. Get insurance to cover employee suits.

CUSTOMER-FOCUSED SELLING

*"When you're selling,
you've got to leave behind the
focus on your business and your
products and focus instead on
your customer and your
customer's needs."*

SELL SOLUTIONS, NOT PRODUCTS!

◇

Customer-Focused Selling is not just an adaptation of existing selling techniques to focus more on the customer. Instead, it's a whole new approach that can barely even be called "selling."

Take any sales techniques you have used in the past, and instead of adapting them, throw them out!

Don't even think of this approach as "selling the customer." Think of it instead in terms of helping customers to find solutions that will help them achieve *their* objectives.

Leave *your* objectives, *your* sales goals, and *your* quotas at the door. Instead, adopt the mindset that you are there as an "inside" consultant to help your prospect with the tools (the products or services) that you have available.

FOCUS ON THE CUSTOMER'S NEEDS!

◇

Customer-Focused Selling means NOT focusing on your great products or wonderful services! It means, instead, focusing on the customer's needs.

I know you can't wait to show them to the customer! I know you can't wait to explain to the customer how you think you can help his or her business! I know you can't wait to go into competitive advantages! But you're going to have to wait! If you want to sell the best way possible, you are going to have to wait to start presenting your products or services.

Instead, you need to shine the spotlight on the customer!

First, you need to find out what the customer wants, what the customer cares about, and what objectives the customer is trying to achieve.

EVERY CUSTOMER IS DIFFERENT

◇

Customer-Focused Selling means helping your customer find added value.

You need to be totally focused and immersed in helping your customer. You need to be focusing on how you can deliver as much benefit as possible toward the customer's objectives. And as business today becomes more complex, a salesperson needs to be able to explore and address buyers who have many different concerns.

In selling to retailers, for example, I see salespeople overwhelmingly assuming that the buyer is completely pre-occupied with how well the salesperson's product will sell. But often retailers' concerns are more complex. They may also need to determine how the product will affect their overall product mix; how it will impact their monthly open-to-buy budget; what co-op advertising funds may be available; and how reliable the re-stocking schedule will be.

Today more than ever, each customer has very unique concerns, and you can't sell until you find out what those concerns are!

HAVE A DIALOGUE, NOT A PRESENTATION!

◇

Keep your sales presentation customized to the one customer you are with.

You may very well have a slick dog-and-pony show that's lots of fun to present to customers. Maybe it's a video, a computer program, or just a four-color catalog. Think twice before you make a generic presentation.

Customers don't want to hear about how great your company is or how wonderful your products are. They want to have their concerns answered.

Today, customers are overflowing with information, and they are tired of slick, high-tech presentations.

What you can offer is a presentation that addresses their concerns and issues—and *ONLY* their concerns and issues.

Better yet, think of your "presentation" as a two-way dialogue in which both you and the customer explore the customer's needs first, and then determine how your products or services may be able to meet those needs.

PUT ON YOUR CUSTOMER'S SHOES!

◇

Customer-Focused Selling means imagining yourself in your customer's shoes from the beginning to the end of the sales process.

Wouldn't you rather have a salesperson call on you who genuinely wants to help you find solutions for your business than a salesperson who is just going to blast canned product sales pitches at you?

Wouldn't you rather deal with a salesperson who explores solutions with you instead of tries to close the sale prematurely or who meets every one of your objections with an argumentative response?

Wouldn't you rather deal with a salesperson who is trying to sell you the best product or service for your needs than the one that they can make the most money on?

THINK SUCCESS!

"If you're like me, it might not always come naturally—but you can push yourself to think positive, and to talk success!"

SUCCESS IS ALL IN YOUR MIND!

◇

Thinking success goes a long way toward being a success!
If you picture yourself as someone who is ultimately
going to succeed—then success is going to come a lot easier.

If, on the other hand, you picture yourself as someone
who is either highly likely to fail or not to progress—then no
matter how talented you are or how hard you work, it's
going to be very difficult to succeed.

Thinking success can catapult your career or business
ahead and make you more effective in all kinds of different
situations, from dealing with people, to concentrating on
analytical issues, to developing creative ideas.

Thinking failure can stop you cold, like the icy moat or
cold stone walls of a medieval castle, and make you less
effective in dealing with people, less able to focus on your
work, and less likely to develop creative ideas.

THE SUCCESS FORMULA!

◇

So how can you think success? Here's a few quick suggestions equally applicable if you're running your own business or trying to build a career:

1. Have a five-year plan for success.
2. Realize that *you*, not others, ultimately control your success.
3. Brainstorm alternatives to tough situations.
4. Celebrate your achievements.
5. Shrug off your setbacks.
6. Develop a support network.
7. Always stand for integrity.
8. Remind yourself that every day is a new opportunity!
9. Keep yourself in top physical condition.
10. Always be open to learning new ideas.

SUCCESS MEANS FINDING ALTERNATIVES!

◇

No matter what job you have or what business you are in, a lot of crummy things are going to happen to you along the way.

But your ultimate success is going to have a lot more to do with *how you respond* to setbacks than with the setbacks you actually encounter.

Just a couple of weeks ago, I was blown away when an overhaul of our cash-flow forecasting showed we had underestimated our Fall borrowing needs by 100 percent. I would need to borrow an extra million dollars—close to our limit!

Uncomfortable with this outlook, I spent an entire evening searching for solutions, but emotionally I couldn't get past the bad news—so I couldn't find any solutions. However, the next day I woke up feeling refreshed and optimistic and was able to shave over $400,000 in expenses and add $500,000 in projected new income.

If you have the right attitude, you can always find alternatives.

NO RISK MEANS NO SUCCESS!

◇

To really get ahead, you've got to take some risks. No successful business or career was built without some risk taking.

This doesn't mean you should walk off a cliff—but instead you need to take calculated risks, after you have carefully collected and weighed all the information you can gather.

How much risk should you take? How far ahead do you want to go?

I don't think it's a coincidence that some of the most spectacularly successful business people have also had some spectacular failures and near failures. Take Henry Ford or Thomas Edison, for example; they didn't let their failures hold them back.

Come to think of it, with all of the failures I've had . . . maybe some *really* big success is just around the corner!

SUCCESSFUL PEOPLE CELEBRATE!

◇

An important ingredient for success is celebrating each and every triumph—and forgetting about every failure—both with the people around you and with yourself, too!

This doesn't come naturally to me, but I have a great sales manager who more than makes up for it.

I might be complaining about how disappointed I am that our sales are *off budget* by 15 percent, but then he'll point out how happy he is that sales are *up* 20 percent *over the previous year!* His kind of talk breeds success!

Don Dwyer, the late franchise king, emphasized in his paperback book *Target Success* how important it is to celebrate success even if you don't hit your exact goals. If sales are budgeted to be up 20 percent, but they only went up 17 percent, celebrate anyway! Have a party for the company and give yourself a reward, too!

Me—I just bought an awesome powerboat with a two-hundred-horsepower engine!

THE CHECK IS IN THE MAIL

"If you have to sell on credit, you need to focus on turning those receivables into cash as soon as you possibly can."

WATCH YOUR RECEIVABLES!

$\diamond$

My father spent over thirty years of his career in banking, loaning money to all kinds of small businesses. The advice he gives me more than any other is "Watch your receivables!"

One of the first business terms I learned when I started extending credit to other businesses was "net 30." It really means that if you send out lots of reminder notices and call repeatedly to demand payment, you'll probably get paid in 90 or 120 days.

I recently heard about one firm that puts an "X" mark on each invoice it owes, every time a creditor calls up demanding payment. When a total of three "Xs" have been noted on it, the invoice gets paid.

THE FASTEST WAY TO GET CASH!

◇

My accounting staff includes a full-time credit and collections manager, an accounting manager, and a controller. But I make sure that I'm personally keeping tabs on receivables.

One quick way to get a grasp on the situation is to look at the average days outstanding. Another is to look at an aging summary that shows how much in receivables is less than 30 days outstanding; 30–60 days outstanding; 60–90 days outstanding; 90–120 days outstanding; and over 120 days outstanding.

I'll personally review the aging summary at least once per month. And at least every couple of months, I'll personally review individual problem accounts with the collections manager to make sure that we're being as aggressive as we can be in getting paid.

Collecting overdue bills is almost always the Number one quickest way to improve your cash flow. And the sooner you collect overdue receivables, the better your chance of collecting them at all!

WHEN THEY CAN'T PAY YOU . . .

◇

What do you do when customers say they can't pay you? If you're collecting from an individual or a small business, give the option of paying by credit card. If this doesn't work, ask for a partial payment. Perhaps you can get the customer to agree to a regular payment plan—this often works for us. If you can't get any money today, try to at least get a promise of a specific date on which you can expect to *receive* the check.

What about taking the customer to court? I have successfully collected thousands of dollars in small claims court. But it is a very time-consuming process, and the outcome is never certain. And to go to a regular court, you'll need lots of money for legal fees and lots of patience to wait for your court date.

SPEEDING UP RECEIVABLES

◇

Once a customer has finally decided to pay your bill, it typically takes quite a while to actually get the funds into your account. Ideally what you'd like your customers to do is to wire you payment. I am often able to get overseas customers to pay by wire—this saves not only the time waiting for an overseas letter, but also the extra time banks take to make available funds drawn on foreign banks.

But I'm not able to get my U.S. customers to pay by wire. So for my larger customers, rather than wait for the mail, I'll give them our FedEx or other overnight courier number and have them send payment at our expense.

LOCKBOXES WORK WONDERS!

$\diamond$

One of the most basic ways to speed receivables is to use a bank's lockbox. Instead of customers mailing payments to you, they mail them to the P.O. box of a bank—which some banks may check as often as every hour of the day. The funds go into your account immediately, and then, afterward, the bank sends you the accompanying paperwork so that you can properly credit each payment.

When we switched to a lockbox we also benefited by using a bank in Boston that gets its mail a day or two faster than we did in our small town.

The bank will charge you for a lockbox, so run the numbers to be sure it's financially feasible, but even many very small businesses will find it highly worthwhile.

CREATING A SENSE OF URGENCY

"If you can get your staff really excited about their work and the business as a whole, their performance can absolutely leap ahead!"

GET 'EM FIRED UP!

◇

I bet you know the feeling. You get to work and you're all revved up to do whatever it takes to push up sales, to pound down costs, and to yank up your profits. But you look around your office and notice that other people, while they hope the business succeeds, just don't have the same sense of urgency about them.

I try telling people we need more sales, we need more profits—but such general talk falls on deaf ears.

On the other hand, once you give people some realistic, specific objectives, then they start to listen.

If you give them some micro-goals—things each person can individually do—and show them how it relates to the whole company—they listen more. Give them some responsibility, some room for decision-making—and then you really begin to get them on board.

Remind 'em that they're on a winning team, heap on praise and rewards for positive achievements, and before you know it—they'll be pulling you along!

BRING 'EM TOGETHER!

◇

Sharing information and having some common goals are great ways to create a feeling of unity and a sense of urgency as an organization.

Try a company meeting once a month where you share sales, cost, and profit information. An in-the-flesh meeting adds to the sense of common purpose, direction, and involvement.

Compare the actual results with your goals. Where did you succeed? Where did you not? What can be done better next month?

Unfortunately, my tendency is to focus on what went wrong and who's to blame—*big mistake*!

Single out people who did a great job, not people who blew it.

Even after a bad month, it's up to you to show everyone that you have the energy, positive attitude, and "can-do" enthusiasm to turn the situation around.

DIVIDE UP RESPONSIBILITY!

◇

I f you've got more than six or seven employees, company-wide goals and meetings aren't going to be enough to push a sense of urgency throughout the organization.

You need goals for each work group or even for specific individuals. Get their input, but keep the goals as quantifiable as possible, such as "We'll increase our direct-mail response rate from 2 percent to 3 percent" or "We'll reduce our defect rate from 0.5 percent to 0.4 percent."

To really get people humming, divide up areas of responsibility as widely as possible. For example, if you have three people in your marketing department and you serve three different types of markets like consumer, business, and government, give each marketing person primary responsibility for each one. Don't just have the marketing manager be responsible for all three.

Wal-Mart, for one, has followed this principle, aggressively assigning a lot of responsibility to many department managers at each store, rather than centering decision-making at the store manager level.

FOCUS ON FRESH OBJECTIVES!

◇

If your goal setting is limited to the same kind of objectives every month such as overall sales or cost and profit goals, people's attention will begin to wane.

So from time to time focus on different kinds of goals. Do a product quality review, a customer satisfaction review, or a cost review—or have a new product idea brainstorming meeting.

Try to limit the focus to a few days at most and build some excitement around it.

Consider assigning people into different groups. Encourage suggestions from everyone. Announce prizes for the best suggestions. I find announcing specific contests with specific cash awards even of modest amounts such as $50 or $100 works wonders.

Have a kickoff meeting where you announce specific objectives and a wrap-up meeting where you go out of your way to compliment contributors and hand out prizes.

This is a great way to show everyone that their contribution matters and that anyone can contribute new ideas to running the business better.

MORE WAYS TO GET PEOPLE IN MOTION!

—————————— ◇ ——————————

Here are some additional ways to create a positive sense of urgency throughout the organization:

- Tie in monthly, quarterly, or annual bonuses to specific goals.
- Share with all employees how your cost and profit numbers compare with industry averages.
- Pick some of your most direct competitors and benchmark your progress against theirs.
- Get your staff more interested in the industry by taking them to trade shows, passing around trade publications, and talking about industry-wide news.
- Success motivates more success. Talk up how you're all on the winning team and find every reason you can possibly think of to celebrate your success: Five years in business—celebrate! First million-dollar month—celebrate! New product launch—celebrate!

STAYING OUT OF COURT

"Legal problems can not only soak up lots of money, but also the time and energy of key people at your company— so take the extra steps to protect yourself!"

MINIMIZE LEGAL RISKS!

◇

The best way to stay out of court is to avoid problems before they occur. Run your business within the law, treat your employees great, use highly detailed purchase orders, use contracts for major deals with binding arbitration clauses, and keep careful records.

I like to skimp on just about everything in business, but a few extra dollars spent up-front on the best lawyers you can find, I have learned the hard way, will save a lot of money down the road. Don't use a general attorney for your business. Use a business attorney or, better yet, a major firm that's highly experienced in your industry. I'm still bound by some below-industry-standard-quality contracts from our early days when we had a good business lawyer, but one who did not specialize in book publishing. And don't hesitate to seek a specialist especially for employment law–where every day current court decisions are significantly changing the law.

EARLY RESPONSES AVERT SUITS

◇

I n many potentially litigious situations, an early
response may avert a suit. Often legal claims arise out
of misunderstandings, which a one-on-one discussion
can resolve.

For example, if you have decided not to pay a bill
because of a quality issue, call the supplier immediately. Try
to win allies within the supplier's company—like the sales
rep—to argue your case for you. Simply not paying the bill,
without promptly apprising the vendor of the problem, is
begging for trouble.

Similarly, if a customer is not happy with goods or
services you supplied, face the real problem head-on, don't
just turn the account over to a collection agency.

Similarly, if an employee has a legitimate complaint
about a sexually hostile work environment issue, investigate
the matter promptly—but also make sure you don't trample
on the rights of the alleged perpetrator.

TRY A SETTLEMENT MEETING

◇

I f you're not making any progress with phone calls and letters in resolving a business dispute, you may want to try a settlement meeting.

I refused to pay a bill because a vendor had not met an agreed-upon delivery schedule. My purchasing people and I had numerous meetings and calls with representatives of the other firm at all levels from sales rep to president. I was sure that we would not be able to get anywhere without going to court.

But my attorney convinced me to arrange a formal settlement meeting with principals, experts, and attorneys. Not only were we able to settle the case for much less than I thought we would, but in listening to the other side, I was surprised to see the validity of many of their arguments.

CONSIDER BINDING ARBITRATION

◇

I f you have a business dispute that you just can't resolve through discussion, you may want to take it to binding arbitration. In this case both parties agree on an arbitrator (often a retired judge) through an arbitration organization and agree that the results of the arbitration will be binding in court.

Certainly consult with your attorney before taking this step–if the facts weigh in your favor and the amount of the dispute is significant, you may very well do better in a court of law.

SOMETIMES COURT IS THE BEST OPTION

◇

While you generally want to stay out of court, there are some situations where filing suit is your best option.

For example, we licensed the content of a book to a very large software company that went way beyond the bounds of the license, trampling all over our rights. We talked over a period of time with the company's lawyers, but they offered us just a token settlement.

However, two days after we filed a claim in court, the president of the company called me and we quickly hammered out a more appropriate settlement.

Don't be intimidated by the size of the company that has wronged you, but do compare its financial resources to yours. With your attorney, do a careful analysis of the risk versus the cost of suing, and make your decision.

FRAUDS, SCAMS, AND RIP-OFFS

*"Don't be paranoid of crooks
and thieves lurking around
every corner—but keep in the
back of your mind a little sense
of when you need to be careful."*

THE CLASSIC "CUSTOMER" FRAUD

◇

Is your new customer a fraud? Years ago, I received an order for books from a library wholesaler in Michigan. Since he had limited credit and bank references, I shipped his first order on a COD basis. Then he placed a much larger order worth several thousand dollars. I again insisted on COD payment—but we never got paid. No—the check didn't bounce; he stopped payment on it—which made it more difficult for us to get legal authorities to help us. Eventually enough publishers were ripped off that he was prosecuted, convicted, and put in jail. I heard he had converted his assets to gold bars—but I never saw a penny.

This is a common pattern in fraud cases—when the criminal pays for a small quantity of merchandise to build your confidence and then later places an order and tries to disappear with a much larger amount.

WHAT NUMBER DID YOU DIAL?

◇

Does your business use an answering machine on its phone lines during off-hours? A couple of years ago, an operator of a phone-sex service reprogrammed our corporate answering machine to direct all of our off-hour incoming calls on our 800 telephone number to the sex service!

This is not an uncommon scam—often larger corporations with busier phone lines are targeted! Amazingly, all of the phone companies we contacted said that they had no recourse against the phone-sex operator. While this kind of scam may not cost you a lot of money, it certainly can be embarrassing!

THE BIGGEST RIP-OFF!

◇

The World Wide Web is becoming the biggest business rip-off of the decade! A lot of corporations are spending huge amounts of money on Web access only to have many of their employees spend their time getting sports scores, playing games in cyberspace, and visiting sites sponsored by adult magazines.

But a lot more money is being lost by smaller companies and entrepreneurs who think that they can make a killing by selling products on the Web. For the foreseeable future, this is a pipe dream! Today, the only people making money on the Web are promoters selling "get-rich-quick seminars" and consultants who build the sites. On our main Web site (careercity.com), for example, even with traffic of 150,000-plus hits a day, some days we don't even get a single order for a book or software package.

FRAUD RUN RAMPANT!

———————— ◇ ————————

If you're thinking of responding to a business opportunity ad—watch out! Fraud and rip-offs run rampant! If it sounds too good to be true—like "Make $35,000 a year part-time stuffing envelopes"—don't touch it!

Hot businesses today—including 900 telephone number services and computer-related businesses—are ones to be particularly careful of. I have heard of people investing $25,000 in a computer-related business and still having no idea how to go out and get customers!

Check to see if the Better Business Bureau or your state's consumer protection office knows anything about the business. But remember—government agencies are generally very slow to respond and shut down business opportunity scams. So take the matter into your own hands and visit plenty of current operators before you invest a penny!

IS IT REALLY AN INVOICE?

◇

As a manager, you're too astute to fall for most mail frauds, but do you open all the mail and okay all the payables?

More and more businesses are sending out marketing pieces designed at first glance to look either like invoices or official government correspondence.

And then there are the real scam artists. For example, my office received an invoice for a $425 subscription to a secretary's magazine, for a woman who no longer works at the company.

From time to time, I receive a copy of the infamous Nigerian letter that explains how I can make a fortune by helping some Nigerian business people avoid currency controls. All I have to do is give these people access to my bank account. Amazingly, hundreds of people have lost millions of dollars to this long-lived scheme.

PERKING UP YOUR PACKAGING

*"One of the easiest ways
to bump up your sales is
to spruce up your packaging!"*

PACKAGING CAN MEAN EVERYTHING!

———————— ◇ ————————

"**D**on't judge a book by its cover," they say—but as a book publisher I can tell you that the cover is exactly how most people judge books! Especially when you're selling a product through retailers, the name of the product, the design of the package, and the sell copy make all the difference in the world!

The first resume book I published was called *Paper Tiger* and sported a cover picture of the same animal. The sales were abysmal. We retitled it *The Resume Handbook*, gave it a powerful all-type cover, and bingo—the sales took off!

When we first launched our business software line, the sell-through was weak, and most blamed the packaging— which I found hard to believe since I had designed it myself. Unbeknownst to me, others in my office came up with a great new design—which I finally agreed to try—and our software sales increased markedly.

CREATIVE PACKAGING SELLS!

◇

I f you've got an MBA like me, you're going to be tempted to stick with very standard-shaped packaging—on paper the numbers will always look better. Not only does it take less time to design and have a lower die cost, but you can run it on with your other standard designs and have great economies of scale.

But when you walk around a retail store, it's the odd-shaped packages that stand out and get attention.

A few years ago I published a book called *365 TV-Free Activities That You Can Do with Your Child*. The contents was not much different than that of several hundred other books on kids' activities. But the packaging really stood out. We went for a very small format, just 4 × 6 inches, with a very high page count, 480 pages, making it look almost square, more like a toy than a book. We sold over 500,000 copies.

MAKE THE PACKAGE POP!

---◇---

W hen in doubt on packaging, I'd go bright and brassy rather than light and classy!

It's so important to stand out on that retail shelf and get noticed! If your product is picked up first, the buyer will spend more time with it and be more likely to buy it than the next product he or she looks at.

A buyer at a national chain told us that he loved our packages because they were bright, easy to find on the shelf, and looked lively and accessible. Unfortunately, he also told other publishers to go out and copy what we were doing.

HOW GOOD IS YOUR PACKAGING?

◇

I t is hard to do great packaging, and sometimes, because you're so close to it, it's hard even to know if your packaging is good or not.

For years after starting our business, I thought our packaging was great. Our customers and sales reps never said anything—after all, they were used to it, and it wasn't too much worse than what other small, struggling publishers did. But as I began to try to line up new distribution overseas, the Australians and the Canadians were very candid with me: "You need new packaging!" they told me.

Since then I've gone crazy on design. I hired a super-talented designer with an ad agency background. Now we budget two designers for every book cover, and sometimes we'll go through dozens of cover designs for a single important book.

SKYROCKET SALES WITH POP DISPLAYS!

———————— ◇ ————————

Whatever your package looks like, you can really crank up your sales with point-of-purchase (POP) merchandising.

Free-standing floor displays, usually called "dumps," are perhaps the most powerful point-of-purchase item you can develop. The drawback is that even small runs made out of cardstock can be expensive because of the tooling expense. So unless your product is hot, retailers aren't going to order enough to justify dumps.

Counter displays, called "prepacks" if they double as a self-shipper, are perfect for the small impulse items a retailer might place on a counter.

There are many other point-of-purchase alternatives including posters, tent cards, buttons, and stickers—but I find that dumps and prepacks are by far the best bet.

BUILD YOUR BUSINESS ON THE WEB!

"A Web site is a great way to better service and market to current customers, but often a difficult way to attract new ones."

GO ON-LINE INCREMENTALLY!

———————————— ◇ ————————————

There are a lot of companies spending a lot of money on elaborate World Wide Web sites only to be frustrated with the small amount of revenue their site is generating. Despite the so-called success stories you read about, very few companies are making money on their Web sites.

So if you're considering a Web site for your firm, take an incremental approach. Start with a very simple site and gradually expand it, keeping careful track of your revenue, your costs, and how much your current customers are using the site.

Even a very small service business today should consider a simple Web site—that I would call "an expanded business card." Keep the graphics simple, but have a few paragraphs of text that explain what your business does and why prospects should do business with you instead of your competition.

Even without programming skills you can create a few basic Web pages yourself using off-the-shelf software. Your only ongoing cost will be about $50 a month to a Web access provider.

FOCUS ON CURRENT CUSTOMERS FIRST!

◇

Once you've got a simple Web site up and you're looking to expand it, I'd next focus on providing more information primarily for current customers. Businesses on the Web have had a lot more success serving current customers better and more efficiently than attracting new ones.

The Web can be particularly effective for many kinds of service support. You can provide information twenty-four hours a day, seven days a week, without having anyone on staff. And you can update information instantly.

You might be able to slash your customer-service costs dramatically by shifting customers to the Web. Consider announcing the Web address automatically to all incoming callers on your customer-service line.

For minimal cost, you could just list by category answers to frequently asked questions or solutions to common problems. Later you may want to go to the expense of having a database and search engine added.

PUT YOUR CATALOG ON THE WEB!

◇

Consider putting your product or service catalog on your Web site.

Adding additional pages to your Web site is a fraction of the cost of printing and mailing more catalog pages to even a few thousand customers. So on your Web site you can afford to provide more in-depth information and information on more obscure products that are of interest to only a small portion of your customer base.

If most of your customers have Web access, you may want to shorten, simplify, or even eliminate your printed catalog and direct your customers to an on-line catalog on your Web site—saving a lot of money in printing and mailing costs.

A word of caution: On the Web, your competitors will usually be among your most frequent visitors.

BUILD TRAFFIC FOR YOUR WEB SITE!

◇

Once you have even a modest amount of information on your Web site, you'll want to start using it to attract new business.

It costs nothing but a little time and effort to build traffic to your Web site. Hot links from one site to the next is what the World Wide Web is all about—and these free links (not paid advertising) is how most traffic is created on the Web.

Start with the major search engines and visit their sites for instructions on how to submit your site for free inclusion with their listings.

By using your imagination and the search engines, try to think of related sites from which you might be able to attract customers. E-mail the Webmaster and consider offering a reciprocal link on your site.

If you have a local service business, maybe you can find a community, association, or newspaper-owned site serving your community. If you have a retail business, maybe some of your manufacturers will list you on their sites.

JAZZING UP YOUR WEB SITE!

◇

Although a pretty simple Web site is the best bet for most businesses, there is no limit to how complex and expensive Web sites can be.

One route larger Web sites have taken is to add a lot of "editorial" type of information, becoming more like on-line magazines than just a catalog for their products.

More information and constantly changing information and graphics help build repeat traffic—but it does take time and energy.

You can jazz up your Web site with animation, such as blinking lights and moving cartoons, but the animation may only be visible on more advanced Web browsers. Or you can even add videos and audios—but they will require users to have plug-ins downloaded from other third-party Web sites.

On the other hand, there are still a lot of Web users with very slow modems—so you may want to give users the option of a text-only version of your Web site—or they might never see it at all.

MAKING BUSINESS TRAVEL FUN!

"If you give just a little bit of creative thought to your travel plans—you can end up having a great time—and coming home with lots of positive energy!"

ADDING ADVENTURE TO YOUR TRAVEL!

———————————— ◇ ————————————

Almost everyone who travels for business seems to complain about it, which is really too bad because business travel can be fun!

Last year I went on an intensive thirty-city book tour, packed with media interviews and seminars often starting at five in the morning and ending at nine at night—but I had a great time!

In every city I tried to do something interesting and different even on busy days. Otherwise I find that if you sit in your hotel room at the end of the day you feel tired, bored, and anxious to get home. But if you go to the theater, a horse show, a jazz club, a museum, a unique store—suddenly your whole trip seems more like an adventure and less like another long business meeting.

FEELING AT HOME ON THE ROAD

◇

Another thing that works for me in making business travel fun is trying to catch up with old business acquaintances or friends along the way.

Suppose you don't have friends in cities you're going to? Then bring your own!

Last year, particularly when I was going to be away for weeks at a time, I had my wife and kids meet me a couple of times in distant cities. Not only did we all have a lot of fun— but the kids saw a lot of historical sites as well. In fact, they keep asking when they can go on a trip again. To be sure, I probably wouldn't again take my three- and five-year-old to appointments in the Congressional Office Building, which they confused with an indoor playground, but overall the trips they joined me on were a big success.

Perhaps the most important aspect of having your family join you even on an occasional business trip is that you are more likely to defray the tension or resentment that often builds when one parent or spouse is frequently away on business travel.

STAYING HEALTHY AWAY FROM HOME

◇

Part of the problem with business travel is that you often end up feeling tired, feeling run-down, or actually getting sick. This isn't any fun at all! But usually it is avoidable!

It is particularly important when traveling to exercise, eat, and sleep as regularly as you can. Air or car travel, long meetings, time-zone changes, and heavy food all work against you—so you need to go out of your way to stay healthy!

Exercise is particularly important because when traveling you tend to spend lots of time sitting—on planes, in cars, in waiting rooms, and at meetings. Try to find hotels with pools or exercise rooms, or just exercise in your room. Twenty minutes of exercise at least three hours before bedtime is going to help you sleep better and feel more full of energy.

Don't overeat! Today it's more socially acceptable to order light meals even at business meetings and to order decaffeinated coffee instead of an extra after-dinner drink.

SUCCESS STRATEGIES FOR AIR TRAVEL

◇

For travel by plane, I think the most important rule is to have low expectations. Don't expect to arrive on time . . . and don't count on your plane leaving on time. Otherwise you'll be a constantly disappointed traveler.

And never, ever, check your bags! Pack your bags as lightly as you possibly can or get bags with wheels if you can't easily lift them.

Avoid the big airports. Fly out of Newark instead of Kennedy, Providence instead of Logan, Baltimore instead of National. Big airports mean traffic on the ground and traffic in the sky—increasing your chances of being locked in holding patterns.

Don't drink alcoholic beverages in flight—they'll tire you right out—but drink some water, soda, or juice throughout each flight, especially long flights.

Finally, when the plane arrives, don't jump up and stand in the aisle for five or six minutes. Instead, relax in your seat with a magazine and stroll off the plane with a smile on your face after the crowd has dispersed.

TAKE THE TRAIN FOR A CHANGE!

— ◇ —

For travel between major northeastern U.S. cities and especially in Europe, I highly recommend train travel.

On a few routes, like Boston to New York, or New York to Washington, travel time on a train city-center-to-city-center is comparable to flying because of the time spent going back and forth to airports.

But even when the travel time may be a little longer, I still prefer the train. I arrive relaxed, and I get more work done on the train than I do when working in my office. Even the coach seats on the train are as big as first-class seats on a plane. Club service on many routes provides a half-decent meal.

Like planes, trains do often run late, but there are side benefits. If, like me, you have a model railroad in your basement, you can get new ideas of what to model—or if you don't, you can just enjoy the scenery.

CHOOSE THE RIGHT SALES FORCE!

"One of the most crucial decisions you make is how to sell your products or services."

CHOOSING SALES-FORCE ALTERNATIVES

—————— ◇ ——————

There are basically four different alternatives for building a sales force:

1. You can hire a larger company or a distributor to sell for you.
2. You can hire independent manufacturers' reps.
3. You can hire your own outside salespeople.
4. You can hire inside or use phone salespeople.

Which choice you make will have a huge impact on your ability to generate sales and, also, your cost structure.

Often the best solution is to use a combination of the different sales models. For example, we use distributors abroad and in specialty markets; our own sales managers for the largest book and software accounts; manufacturers' reps for midsize accounts; and phone selling for the smallest accounts.

USE SOMEONE ELSE'S SALES FORCE!

◇

Especially if you have a small product business, you're probably going to be better off trying to get a larger company or a distributor to sell your goods.

Even if you could get sales reps or manufacturers' reps to sell your product, it may be difficult to persuade companies to open a new account for you, and getting paid may tax your patience.

Remember, you need a distributor with an outside sales force who will call on customers and push your product—not a wholesaler who typically stocks a very broad group of manufacturers and more or less waits for customers to send in orders. The terms "wholesaler" and "distributor" are often confused, and it's difficult to judge how aggressively a distributor will push your products—so get references!

MANUFACTURERS' REPS BUILD BUSINESSES!

---◇---

Manufacturers' reps played a crucial role in building my book business and a lot of other businesses. They are paid on commission, so you're not stuck with a high overhead for salaries and travel when sales are low, and they already have an entree with the prospects to whom you need to sell.

Generally a manufacturer's rep sells a lot fewer product lines than a distributor does and will push each line harder.

But it's up to you not just to find reps, but to really *sell them* continually on how hot your products are. Meet with them in person; tell them sales success stories; send them media clippings; send them sales samples; and pay them promptly.

SALES FORCE!

—— ◇ ——

I hired my first salesperson to sell advertising for a tiny map business I started while still in college. I told her to call in every day with a progress report. Three weeks later she first called in and reported nobody was interested. She had lost her call reports, and she needed her paycheck!

Believe me, it's not easy starting up an outside sales force. It's the most difficult and expensive sales solution by far, but the results can be great *if* it all clicks together.

If you decide to hire outside salespeople, you'll need to pay a base salary, not just commission, and keep real close tabs on them. For one, you want to make sure they're really working. And for two, even if they are highly experienced, you need to keep motivating them.

INSIDE SALES IS EASIER TO MANAGE!

◇

Managing and motivating inside or phone salespeople is a lot easier than putting together an outside sales force. You can contact a lot more prospects for a lot less money, and you'll save a lot of money by avoiding travel costs.

Hire people who are articulate. Test them by role-playing a sales scenario before you bring them on board. Pay them an hourly or weekly base wage plus a bonus based on results. In addition, consider impromptu contests like "The next sale gets an extra $25 or a pair of movie tickets!"

If you really need to close sales in person, you may want to have phone salespeople find and qualify leads, and then send a more experienced salesperson, or yourself, to close the sale.

GETTING ROCK-BOTTOM COSTS

"A really low cost structure gives you plenty of leeway for making errors—which is particularly important if you're going to make anywhere near as many mistakes as I have!"

LOW COSTS ALLOW ROOM FOR MISTAKES!

───────── ◇ ─────────

A really low cost structure is one of the most important competitive weapons a business can have at its disposal. It has certainly been important for me. For years my business was terribly undercapitalized, and I was often testing my bank's patience. On top of that, I was always making mistakes. Ad campaigns that didn't sell, products that the market spit back at us, a customer who one year returned virtually all of a half-million dollars in purchases, even entire business units that failed—you name the mistake, I probably made it and more than once!

But our low cost structure gave us a lot of leeway for making errors, and it still allowed us to make money and repay our bank loans, more or less when they were due.

NARROWLY FOCUS YOUR COST REVIEWS!

◇

To get competitive advantage of a low cost structure, I don't mean a percentage point or two below the industry average. I mean ten or fifteen percentage points below.

From time to time you should carefully examine every single cost you incur. Not all at once—it's too overwhelming. But instead, review costs in one small part of your business at a time.

Don't just focus on renegotiating prices or getting more bids. Think about every way possible to reduce the cost or, ideally, eliminate it altogether. You'll find that if you focus on just one item at a time, you'll often be able to come up with some really creative solutions.

Running a small company, I never had much purchasing power with vendors—but in hindsight it was probably to my advantage, since I was forced to focus on more creative, and potentially more substantial, ways to reduce costs.

FOUR STEPS TO LOWER COSTS

◇

Here's a simple four-step process for lowering costs:
1. Try to redesign the product or process to eliminate the cost entirely.
2. Try to change the specs to reduce the costs to the vendor supplying the goods or service.
3. Try to standardize the specifications or change the delivery schedule to increase volume buying capability.
4. Seek bids and negotiate.

Last year in the book industry, paper prices skyrocketed. We tried to eliminate paper altogether by launching electronic products. For books, we changed our paper specifications, typically from fifty- to thirty-five-pound paper, saving 30 percent in tonnage. Finally, we began buying paper by the carload and negotiated prices aggressively.

LOWER COSTS IS NOT JUST NEGOTIATING!

◇

It's hard to get other people to shift their cost-control efforts beyond price negotiation.

For example, my operations manager used to perennially complain about the increasing price of cardstock, trying to get me ready to accept an increase in his box budget. I knew he was doing a great job negotiating prices, but our costs were still poised to rise, and I don't like rising costs.

So I pushed him to look for additional solutions, such as reusing more of the boxes printers used to ship books to us, changing the assortment of boxes we use, and substituting padded envelopes for boxes on smaller-sized shipments.

At the same time, my marketing department was spending more and more money on counter displays—all of which we ship inside cardboard boxes. So I encouraged my marketing and operations managers to get together and design prepacks or self-shippers in order to eliminate the cost of a separate shipping box.

PRICES ARE ALWAYS NEGOTIABLE!

◇

H ere are a few suggestions that have worked for me in negotiating lower prices:

- Get lots of competing bids for exactly the same specs.
- Set a target price. For example, when buying a year-long service that had a standard price of $25,000 per month, I told the vendor we'd pay $10,000, period. We saved $180,000.
- Change the classification. In buying advertising from a huge media corporation that is notorious for not going off their rate card, I nonetheless insisted on a special deal. They got my business by creating a whole new low-rate category for which only our firm qualified.
- Charm the people at the vendor you are buying from— get them on your side, pushing the decision makers for a lower rate.
- Demonstrate that you will definitely buy now, given a great price.
- Always be prepared to walk if you don't get exactly the deal you want.

POLICIES AVOID PROBLEMS!

"Established and publicized policies tend to deflate potential arguments with employees over accepted procedures."

WHY YOU NEED POLICIES

—— ◇ ——

I f you're starting a small business, you may think, "I don't need employment policies . . . that's the kind of bureaucratic nonsense that I'll leave to the big corporations." Well, that's what I thought when I went into business, but I soon found that a few basic policies help avoid arguments, and misunderstandings, and decrease your chances of losing lawsuits.

When you have more than a dozen employees, I'd recommend you create an employee handbook that lays out in clear, simple language what is and isn't acceptable in the workplace and that outlines grievance procedures.

But don't throw together an employee handbook yourself unless you're willing to spend the money to hire an attorney who specializes in employment to review it.

Company handbooks have been seen by the courts as legally binding contracts, and employees have successfully sued companies for not honoring their own handbooks.

SEXUAL HARASSMENT IS A HOT ISSUE!

◇

Sexual harassment should be a very real concern for every business manager and owner in the country. There are many people—overwhelmingly women—who are legitimate victims of sexual harassment.

As an owner or manager you're responsible for not only your actions, but the actions of everyone who reports to you. By the so-called reasonable woman standard your workplace may be deemed "a sexually hostile environment" because of sexually oriented actions, jokes, pictures, or language.

Many companies are victims of sexual harassment suits that have little or no merit but are seen by a dismissed or aggravated employee as the easiest way to retaliate.

Even at a small company, you should be able to demonstrate you have a firm policy against sexual harassment and an established procedure for making complaints. Just being completely innocent is not going to make for a rock-solid defense.

EQUAL-OPPORTUNITY ISSUES

———————— ◇ ————————

Everyone in your office should know that you have a policy of equal opportunity for all. It's the law.

This includes undertaking some expenditures if necessary, with the value being dependent upon the size of your company, to employ physically challenged people.

It's particularly important that anyone who will be interviewing job candidates, not just the primary hiring decision maker, be extremely aware of equal-opportunity law and be careful not to ask any questions that might violate it.

A tough question that many businesses face concerns employees who can still make it to work but, because of a deteriorating mental or physical condition, perform their job very poorly. The law requires you to make reasonable accommodations—but just what these reasonable accommodations are is often very difficult to determine. You'll be well advised in these situations to consult with an attorney specialized in employment issues.

FORGET THE DRESS CODE!

◇

hat about a dress code? Should you have one?

If customers or clients frequent your workplace, I'd set a few basic standards for dress such as shirts—not T-shirts; slacks—not jeans; shoes—not sneakers; and skirts—not shorts.

But if you don't have customers in your workplace, I'd skip the formal dress code altogether—except for truly offensive dress such as skimpy outfits or T-shirts with profane messages or pictures. Yes, a liberal dress policy is perhaps going to result in many sloppily dressed employees—but this is the trend in corporate dress, so why not let your employees dress the way they want to.

WORK HOURS, SMOKERS, AND PHONE USAGE

I like to see my employees work regular hours—but I'm liberal if there's a particular reason to be in late, leave early, or take the day off. Especially in this day of dual working parents, I'll also change someone's regular hours if they want, but I do want everyone coming in on a regular schedule. Now, if in addition they want to work nights or weekends—that's okay, too!

What about smokers? I send them outside. Smokers have no legal rights—and my only moral obligation is to do everything I can to discourage them from destroying their lungs!

Personal phone usage can be an issue. Just a few months ago my controller decided to clamp down on it by issuing everyone three-digit codes that had to be entered after every call. People were furious, and we quickly dropped the extra digits! Unless there is a particularly blatant abuser, don't get bent out of shape if people are making a few short, personal phone calls.

BUILDING THE WINNING TEAM

"Everyone wants to feel that they are on a winning team, that the company is moving ahead, and that they are an integral part of the group."

BEYOND HIRING GREAT PEOPLE

◇

Building the winning team requires more than just hiring a bunch of talented people.

It means hiring people who will work well together.

It means developing a shared vision and commitment.

It means physically bringing people together in formal group meetings for open discussion of broad-based issues.

It means encouraging positive, informal interactions between group members.

It means instilling a "winning" attitude throughout the organization.

It means watching for and quickly trying to reverse team-building problems such as jealousy, cynicism, and defensive behavior.

GET 'EM TO "BUY IN"!

◇

To build the winning team, you not only need to show people what direction the company is headed in, but you need to get them to "buy into" this direction. Otherwise, you can't expect people to support a group if they don't agree with where it's headed or, worse, don't even know where it's headed.

Specifically, you need to show people:

- Your vision for the future.
- Your strategy for getting there.
- Why this is the best strategy.
- Every achievement that indicates this team is winning.

This is not a one-time discussion or announcement. You need to constantly remind people what the organization stands for and that it does indeed hold a bright future for them!

MEETINGS BUILD TEAMS

◇

Part of building the winning team is having some group meetings. Meetings, or even parties or celebrations, with as many people as possible from the entire organization, help build a feeling of solidarity throughout the organization.

But it is also important to have everyone participate in smaller group meetings where some work is done or some decisions are made. This makes people feel that they aren't just part of some big group, but that they are an active, important part of a team.

For key managers, or people in your work group, you should have an interactive meeting once per week—not a meeting where you just make announcements and summarize the work that's been done and needs to be done, but a meeting where everyone has an opportunity to give feedback on substantive issues.

GETTING PEOPLE TO WORK TOGETHER

◇

Perhaps the most difficult part of building a winning team is encouraging positive, informal interaction between team members when you are not present. Here are some thoughts on this:

- Have team members take part in the hiring process of new team members.
- Assign specific projects for two team members to work on together.
- Try to arrange for close proximity of offices.
- Create an incentive-pay plan based on common goals such as profitability.
- Have a specific part of the salary review dependent upon "interaction with others."
- Take your team off-site for formal meetings as well as casual get-togethers to build a sense of bonding.

WATCH OUT FOR TEAM DESTROYERS!

◇

Here are some of the problems that can rip the team-building process apart.

Jealousy. Be on guard for jealousy whenever a new member is hired into the group. Go out of your way to tell other team members how much their work is appreciated.

Cynicism. Some people are just negative by nature. Others might feel your company can't possibly prosper or they just don't like small companies, big companies, or whatever.... Be sure you are emphasizing the company's positive achievements to the group as a whole. And don't hesitate to confront any openly cynical individual and demand their behavior change at once.

Lack of confidence. Some people lack confidence in themselves and view attacks on their opinions as attacks on themselves, responding with statements like "Are you telling me my fifteen years of experience don't matter?" Stop any discussion like this immediately and, in a private one-on-one meeting, patiently point out the defensive behavior.

SAVING THE TROUBLED BUSINESS

"Sooner or later you're going to face a business crisis—don't worry, it's seldom as bad as it seems, and chances are very unlikely you'll have as many crises as I've had!"

HANDLING BUSINESS CRISES

◇

Maybe a huge new competitor is attacking you head-on, or maybe your bank is reducing your credit line, or maybe your fast growth is outpacing your capital base—in any event, sooner or later, a lot of businesses, especially small, fast-growing businesses, face a serious financial crisis. Here's how to respond:

1. Don't panic—a financial crisis often first appears worse than it turns out to be.
2. Find out how bad it really is: Do whatever financial analysis you need—most often a new cash-flow projection—to get the facts.
3. Make time to come up with a carefully thought-out action plan before you take any drastic steps.

THE LIFEBLOOD OF THE BUSINESS

──────────◇──────────

My ex-banker father reminds me that cash is the lifeblood of any business. In developing a plan to save a financially troubled business, give emphasis first to cash flow and don't hesitate to sacrifice short-term profits or growth.

Categorize which bills you absolutely need to pay and which you can hold off on. Taxes, payroll, utilities, and a few core suppliers need to come first. Hold off on purchases and sell down inventory. If you've got to cut people, then make your first cuts deep enough so that you won't have to cut again—there is nothing worse for morale than successive rounds of layoffs.

TIME TO RE-EVALUATE STRATEGY

—— ◇ ——

A time of financial crisis may not seem like the best time, but you also need to re-evaluate the viability of your business strategy. Has new competition, a changing marketplace, or a deteriorating financial condition made it obsolete? There's no sense in going through a lot of cost cutting and other financial quick fixes if the underlying issues that led to the crisis are not being addressed.

For example, I see many independent retailers who, when threatened by a competing "superstore" whose main appeal to the public is a huge assortment of inventory, respond by actually cutting their own inventory to build cash reserves. In so doing, the independent retailers hasten their own demise.

DEVELOP AN ACTION PLAN!

◇

Once you've evaluated how serious the financial crisis is and re-evaluated your business strategy, you need to develop a detailed action plan including new budget, profit-and-loss, cash-flow, and balance-sheet projections. Particularly if you're running a very small business you're probably thinking, "Well, that's easy for him to say, but I'm struggling just to keep up with the day-to-day demands of running this business—where do I get the time to put together a new plan?"

Believe me, I've been there. And all that day-to-day struggle in any small business is a waste of time if you are not operating according to an up-to-date plan. Otherwise, your business is out of control and you are no longer managing it.

BENEFITS OF GOING THROUGH A CRISIS

$\diamondsuit$

Turning around a financially troubled business probably doesn't sound like a lot of fun—making lots of cutbacks during the day and spending most of the night cranking out new financial projections. But taking a proactive approach to guiding a business through a financial crisis can have its benefits:

- You can shed many unnecessary costs.
- You can get employees rallied around a specific cause.
- You can open people's minds to new directions.
- You can create a sense of unity and purpose.
- You can instill a feeling of vigor and excitement.

AVOIDING THE BIGGEST BUSINESS BLUNDERS!

"If you can avoid just a few of the biggest, most crucial mistakes that I've made—success is going to come much easier."

YOU'VE GOT TO BE REALLY DIFFERENT!

◇

No matter how talented you are in business, you're going to make mistakes. But if you can avoid just a few of the biggest, most crucial mistakes that I've made, success is going to come a whole lot easier.

In several different businesses, I completely torpedoed any chance of success by making direct frontal attacks at established businesses, competing for the same customers in the same way. For example, I started a free newspaper offering general "Help Wanted" ads, competing more or less head-on with Boston's big newspaper, the *Boston Globe*. Guess who won?

At the MBA programs they call this "strategy," but it's just as easy to think of it as being "different." Not just a little better—but really different! With my newspaper, I could have gone for a particular market segment—like technical help. Or perhaps I could have tried something really different like running job fairs or collecting resumes of job candidates and selling access to them.

NEVER LOOK AT AN EXPENSE IN ISOLATION!

◇

I t's so easy to make blunders handling money in a business. But my biggest mistakes come about when I don't keep looking at the budget and the cash-flow projection.

Every day in business you are bombarded with what seems like great reasons to spend money on something you didn't budget. You get ideas from ads, salespeople, employees, even your relatives!

Taken in isolation, so many unplanned expenses seem like a great idea! Think how fast a new computer would be! Wouldn't new desks look sharp!

But when I start to make even one or two exceptions a week to my budget, I soon find my budget and profit projection were just a fantasy.

WALK BEFORE YOU LEAP WITH MARKETING!

◇

I could talk about my marketing blunders forever—but the bottom line is clear. You never know what is going to work in marketing, so don't be afraid of making lots of mistakes—as long as they are *small* mistakes!

- Never, ever, spend lots of money on any marketing program until you see that it is bringing in money.
- Never assume that someone else's marketing program will work for you.
- Never assume that an ad agency or marketing expert can guarantee you results—no one can.
- Make small test promotions and put in that extra effort to carefully measure results.
- Ask every customer how they heard about your business, and track the response to every promotional effort.

There are some marketing avenues out there that will work for your business—but it could take you a long time to find the right mix of the right media, the right offer, the right ad copy, and the right ad design.

SPRING FOR THE COFFEE!

———— ◇ ————

Everyone makes some big blunders managing people, and I've made more than my share. A lot of business owners and newly minted managers tend to be too harsh and demanding—like me!

At one of my first ventures in college, a housepainting business, even my employees would give me free people-management advice. I remember one of them saying, "Hey, Bob, how come you can't act like a normal guy and spring for coffee and doughnuts now and then?" I grudgingly started taking five bucks out of my wallet and ten minutes out of each workday for the coffee break, but in higher productivity I probably made back the money many times over.

Obviously, buying the coffee is only a starting place in treating people right. I've found that you can't just drive people to work 100 percent flat out all day long and well into the night—well, at least not every day! So even if people are doing a reasonably good job—loosen up and show them how much you appreciate their work!

NURTURE RELATIONSHIPS WITH KEY CUSTOMERS!

◇

Dealing with customers is something I never seem to get right. Like so many businesses, we spend too much effort on making the sale and not enough on building the relationship. This would be fine if nothing changed or there were never any major problems—but there always are.

You are so much better off if you have developed a close relationship with key decision-makers, and not just the buyers at businesses with which you are dealing. Sooner or later I find that there will be some kind of problem—such as overdiscount, payment terms, faulty products, or whatever—and you're going to end up dealing with the key decision makers for the first time under negative circumstances.

Even if you're a relatively small vendor, you may be surprised how receptive executives of a large company you're doing business with may be to meet with you, especially if they know you are not just meeting with them to simply get more orders, but to try to serve their needs better.